HOUSE & GARDEN'S COMPLETE GUIDE TO
INTERIOR DECORATION

SEVENTH EDITION
BY THE EDITORS OF HOUSE & GARDEN

SIMON AND SCHUSTER / NEW YORK / 1970

Edited by Harriet Burket, former Editor-in-Chief of *House & Garden*
Associate Editor, Collette Richardson
Book designed by Audrey R. Flamberg

CONTENTS

Old and new blend in a bare-floored white room spiked with a dash of purple.

GRIGSBY

THE TEMPO AND TEMPER
OF THE WAY WE LIVE TODAY

Home can and should be a very personal place, but it is bound to reflect the world in which we live. Today's interiors are different from those of our parents because the world around us is different from theirs. Probably the two factors that have effected the biggest changes are lack of household help and lack of space. Both, at first glance, seem negative, but they have worked to our advantage by giving us more honest values and tastes, and better techniques. With the disappearance of trained domestics, for example, many pretentious and meaningless social forms have also disappeared. We have become more sincerely, and less formally, hospitable. Manufacturers and designers have come to our rescue with superbly efficient appliances, cook-and-serve devices, wipe-clean materials and fabrics, to spare us long hours of food preparation, pot-watching, dish washing, laundering and housecleaning. Your rooms may be furnished with rare antiques, but the curtain and upholstery fabrics can now have a protective finish, the Aubusson can be moth-proofed, and the Sheraton four-poster can be equipped with a feather-light mattress and fitted sheets. We live with a companionability that was unknown in an earlier day. We no longer want or have huge, wasted halls, dark basement kitchens, high-ceilinged pantries. Fewer dividing walls, more glass to open up outside walls, planned privacy, organized built-in storage where it is most needed, double-duty rooms and furniture all allow us to enjoy an expansive life in easily maintained surroundings.

It is now possible to see and hear the news in the making, to be entertained by top performers, to listen to any kind of music we like, without leaving the house, so we want a relaxed environment that really caters to us rather than one designed to impress. We want conveniences such as a handy drink-mixing setup, a table ready for other games as well as bridge, deep and well-lighted chairs beside bookshelves, a home office, a hobby corner. We travel farther and more easily than any generation has before, and have learned to appreciate the artistry and craftsmanship of other lands. We bring home (or buy right here) such delights as Portuguese and Greek rugs, Italian ceramics, German and French porcelain, iridescent silks from Asia and India. We assemble collections and enjoy living with them. Efficiency is no longer equated with sterility. Kitchens function ideally yet look very personal, and bathrooms have overtones of splendor that enhance their nerve-soothing, healthful, new properties.

Whatever the decorative approach to your house may be, attune its tempo and its temper to the times. Emphasize the richness and individuality of life at home, its capacity to stimulate or soothe; shore up ease with unobtrusive modern technology. That is the very best way to live today.

Decorating today is a distinct adventure, with a great deal of freedom to express yourself as you wish. Dare to be an innovator rather than a follower. Realize that opposites attract: wicker and fur, opulence and bareness, unmatched area rugs in the same room, painted chairs around a dark wood table. These and others give a house character. Use the points made here and on every page to help put new vitality into your surroundings.

The no-period room—a triumph of livability—is here to stay. The interplay of old and new, simple and elegant, sentimental and practical, is the most provocative of all decorating ploys. The no-period room refuses to be stereotyped; it reflects the range of your tastes and imagination rather than a single design period or mood. It recognizes the validity of placing a clear glass coffee table on an old needlepoint rug, of partnering a mixture of antiques with contemporary pictures, of covering a Louis XV chair in a bold houndstooth check. Wake up your house with this new, uninhibited harmony.

Dominant and daring paintings have a power that will not be denied and a liberated quality that is challenging, devoid of sentimentality, and exciting to live with. Bring fine contemporary pictures into your house and give them an opportunity to speak for themselves in today's terms.

A concentration of many patterns in one place is yet another freedom that flourishes today. Maybe it was sparked by the paintings of Vuillard and Matisse or by the profusion of ornamentation that turns Indian mosques and palaces into fantasies. Whatever the inspiration, we are fascinated by overstatement, revel in its sheer exuberance and find it great fun to live with a pride of patterns.

The sum of a collection is greater than its parts when you use those parts to create one arresting grouping. A concentration of artfully arranged objects attracts the eye at once and invites closer inspection of each item. Abundance is a characteristic of our times and one of its manifestations is our delight in displaying well-composed collections.

Color is unlimited creative currency that is always available to you; its worth depends on how you use it. An extravagance or economy of hue, a splurge of brilliance or neutrality or both, can be an inspired investment. All colors are up-to-date. Use and combine them deliberately—to saturate or highlight, establish a mood, play up architecture and furnishings or fade them out. Be wise but openhanded with color; spend it generously at home.

An easy alliance (right), of formal antiques, rush and wicker baskets, three fabrics, groups of old porcelain against glazed walls

**A living room tapestried with paintings
and rich with small sculptures
is kept calm—to give art precedence.**

Exotic orchids and a bold painting reign together, viewed from caned chairs in a no-period room.

GRIGSBY

A linear composition of facing sofas and massive wall banquettes in white, slashed with blue

INTERIOR DESIGN: MAC II   MASSEY

Densely patterned walls and window shades of
Indian bedspreads plus more patterns on
pillows are offset by solid blue, green and white.

Sophisticated harmony:
antiques
of many eras;
a group of
modern constructions;
a white, neutral
and
jet-black palette

16

STOLLER

Chapter 1

COLOR POWER

HOW TO PUT IT TO WORK

Color has almost unlimited power—to make us see or overlook, to lift our spirits or ease our tensions, to evoke whatever ambiance or mood we want; the less its intensity, the gentler its impact. The light brights are gay and young. Neutrals are persuasively soothing. But every color is a changeling and takes on different characteristics depending on where it is used, the texture underlying it, other colors that are combined with it and the proportions of each. Any color can stand on its own or merge into a simple or complicated harmony. Versatility is color's other name. People's favorite colors vary as much as their personalities so, when planning a room, explore your own preferences, which may include several, and don't be swayed by someone else's scheme unless it evokes the instant response in you: "That's for me." Recognize that fashions in colors and combinations come and go, but that no color is new; what makes it seem so is the way it is used.

When thinking about a color scheme, decide first what you want it to do. You may be faced with problems such as box-rooms utterly devoid of built-in interest, or mishmash architecture and make-do afterthoughts like closets carved out of room corners, a too-large sofa, a too-small Oriental rug, a handsome screen you want to play up. Whatever your quandary, the purposeful use of color can go a long way toward solving it. Begin your planning with limitations or advantages that challenge you, with a color, printed fabric or rug that delights you, or a group of personal treasures you have collected. Then proceed with conviction, because color can fail you if you don't respect its power. For example, the kinetic excitement of a many-hued theme such as the one in the room, *left*, would turn into chaos without the balancing simplicity of white and neutrals. Again, a neutral scheme can be as dreary as a dirge unless it is vitalized by such tonics as contrasts of light and dark, texture, black or white or both. Take advantage of color's genius for camouflage. It can alter proportions, make a bulky chair look smaller, a narrow room wider, a high ceiling lower. It can emphasize or minimize the importance of anything. The flow of color through adjoining rooms should appear so unstudied that one is scarcely aware of it. The dominating hue in one room might be the least important in another, or a gamut of neutrals against white walls could continue through a door and be played up by colored walls, or one mood could spill over a sill with the same color accents the bright, connecting link. For a closer look at the power of color and how to turn it on, study the following 36 pages. The infinite possibilities of one-, two-, and many-colored themes, whites, accents, neutrals; ways to use color's magic . . . . are explored, explained, pictured.

Supercharged colors, *left,* stamp the mighty force of their personalities on a highly dramatic room that soars many feet to the pine ceiling. Low seating keeps the vivid hues on closely related planes. Rosewood platforms extend beyond the sofa and chaise cushions to form side and end tables. Both the base and pillows of the purple chaise separate in the middle to become a chair-and-table and an ottoman-and-table. Brilliant blue cubes and two scarlet rugs bring opposite ends of the room closer to each other. Simplest of backgrounds: a neutral floor, white walls, bare windows.

MARIS

THE BIG SIX

ON THE COLOR WHEEL; THEIR CHARACTERISTICS AND RANGE OF INFLUENCE

GREEN

Easy to live with and deeply satisfying, it can pull a disjointed room together more than any other color. Green brings the freshness of summer and growing things into a room, the lushness of leafiness. Anyone who has lived with only sand, sea and sky for even a brief time knows the hunger for green to cool the eye. Many greens work well together; nature has set the example by weaving them into an ever-changing harmony. Green runs like a strong theme through the history of decorating, its range reaching from the darkest to the lightest, the grayest to the most intense, the near-yellow to the near-blue hues. *Right:* marvelous use of exhilarating green for a new-minted look.

YELLOW

A near-synonym for southern exposure, clear yellow can fill a room with sun and brightness. It is the lightest of all the major colors and the least demanding. You can have it bland as sweet butter, sharp as a lemon, pungent as mustard or curry. It has an affinity for mellow wood finishes, stone, slate, brick. Like blue, yellow is pleasant on a ceiling—and for the same reason: we are accustomed to turning our faces up to the sun. Yellow in all its variations reacts kindly to white and to the sharp edges and shapings of black. It can be the only color in a room or its only accent, and lends itself to mergers with other hues. For a roomful of yellow and white radiance and warmth, see page 24.

BLUE

Like green, blue is one of nature's dependables, arching in varied moods above our heads, bringing infinite changes in sea and shadow, flowers, birds, berries. The lighter values of blue open up space more than any other color, and blue lowers a ceiling most gracefully, because we are accustomed to a canopy of sky. Turquoise, peacock, aquamarine are all blue-cooled; so are blue-violets and purple-blue. Blue is right out front today, in all its many tones, values and possible teamings. It is particularly effective when combined with white, a clean, chinapattern partnership that never fails. For a saturation of blue, and for an interplay of many blue and white patterns, see page 22.

RED

Red can be brazen or gracious, self-centered or very appealing. It can be earthy on a barn, elegant in a drawing room. Two fullstrength reds are vermilion, which leans slightly toward orange, and crimson, which is a degree cooler and the stripe in our flag. Values stretch from deepest garnet to delicate pink. Although not to be trifled with, you can bend red to your will if you understand its dynamics. The easiest way to use bright red: in small strokes. A bolder role: as one of the major colors in a room scheme. The bravest of all: make red reign supreme. Balance its ardor with white, its intensity with dark wood and black. For an all-out statement in distinguished red, see page 25.

ORANGE

Orange can vibrate with heat or glow with suffused warmth depending upon its intensity. It rarely makes a big splash in the outdoor world, and when it does—as across a sunset sky—its moments of glory are numbered. But the rising moon upon occasion, fruits, flames and flowers give us an acute awareness of the magnetism of orange. For accents, it is invaluable, exhilarating, sharpedged as a knife. In bolder sweeps such as a painted floor, a rug, one wall, it can lift a room sky-high. It can even be an all-out performer if freely frosted with white, tempered with neutrals and darks or black. For a basically orange scheme, kept in bounds by the use of these additives, see page 23.

PURPLE

At its peak, purple is dominating, uncompromising, but off-center in any direction it underwrites a spate of lyrical colors. Flower tones of pink and blue lavenders, a big family of magentas, deep shades of plum, grape, eggplant, give you an enormous palette that is part delicate, part intense, part darkly glowing. Blue purples are the quietest and coolest, red ones the warmest and most lively. Pure purple is a sudden, excellent accent for white, pale green-blues, some pinks. Or it can be one of the undiluted colors in a many-hued scheme. Slightly calmed, it can splurge across walls, a floor, or a fabric. On page 26, a bouquet of lavenders and white brings a garden into the house.

ONE COLOR

FOR HEAD-ON IMPACT

A simple, outspoken, and very fresh way with color: pick one of the Big Six and steep a room in it. Use it in broad sweeps—they tend to make even the most intense hue look pleasantly calm. Rely on white for contrast, for coolness, and to make the color sing with extra sweetness or strength. Depend on black or darks to hold down vibrant hues and keep them in their place. If walls carry the color, bring it out into the room in upholstery, painted furniture, a bedspread. If the rug

carries the color, repeat it at a higher level—on chair seats, at the windows. Use texture—matte, shiny, smooth, deep—to give one color a range of appeals. Pattern in your chosen hue or variations of it, spliced with white, possibly nicked with black, creates yet another change of pace and dimension. Add the glint of metal, glass, mirror, favorite pictures and ornaments to a one-color scheme; look at the finished room and take delight in one color's power to please.

The green of a parrot's feathers, *right,* wraps this bedroom in lilting color and fractures into many more greens for the material that upholsters the four-poster bed, a sofa, and a chair. A room to live in, to laze in, with the glint of tiny lemons among the leaves echoed in one yellow pillow, and the tropic coolness of white shutters at the window, white texture across the floor. Interior design: John FitzGibbons.

GRIGSBY

BLUE

Shining lacquered walls, *left,* of rich incandescent blue, a rug and stair carpeting that echo the same color but with the difference which small pattern adds—establish immediate excitement in a luminous entrance hall. Black doors and the curving sweep of a metal stair rail are unexpected, and heighten the dramatic impact of this very individual foyer.

A splash of patterns, *below,* all blue and white, gives this dining room a delightful liveliness. The chinoiserie design on walls and curtains, the simple plaid used for blinds and chair seats, the lacing of lattice on the rug, bring out the best in each other. Solid blue chair frames and a white chest anchor the dominant colors; mellow wood dining and side tables and a crystal chandelier maintain their classic distinction in a roomful of pattern.

ORANGE

Brilliant color is easy to live with, *below,* when it is handled with assurance. Here, orange—full strength for curtains, love seat and chair—is broken up with white into a flame-stitch-patterned wallpaper. For calmness, interior designer Barbara D'Arcy uses an all-white bedspread and canopy, cube table, textured rug; for depth, rich tones of rosewood and a dark floor; for glitter, glass and steel. The old and new are coupled in this bedroom for provocation.

YELLOW

Three versions, *left*, of a sunny
color bring great vitality and
variety to a living room. A plain
sweep of golden-yellow walls
emphasizes the two yellow and white
patterns—flowing and flowered
for curtains and furniture, strictly
geometric for the rug. Closely related
in color and scale, they link two
seating groups; light Hepplewhite
chairs can be easily moved from one
to the other. Against one wall,
the delight of the unexpected: a
contemporary picture, table, a
bench in Dalmatian-patterned leather.

GRIGSBY

RED

Vivid elegance, *right,* is created
in a library by the fearless use
of red cooled with white and teamed
with such beauties as a red-bordered
Aubusson rug that might have been
specially woven for the room, a lavish
Venetian mirror, and a crystal
chandelier. Comfortable chairs and
crowded bookshelves are an invitation
to take one's ease. The bay window
in this same room, *above,* curves
around a plaid silk-draped table, center
stage setting for a vermeil Hazeltine
boar, a blanc-de-chine temple urn.
Wall brackets are blackamoor
sphinxes with gold earrings. The
carpet on the staircase, *top above,*
carries the red from floor to floor
where it takes part in other schemes.

YEE

LEONARD

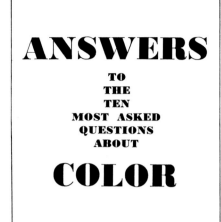

ANSWERS

TO
THE
TEN
MOST ASKED
QUESTIONS
ABOUT

COLOR

Q *When two rooms adjoin, such as a living room and entrance hall, must I use the same scheme for both or is there no absolute rule?*

A There are no hard rules. Your own likes count most. Related colors and patterns, not necessarily identical ones, enhance a feeling of space in adjoining areas. You might let the living room's accent hue dominate in the hall, or use one patterned fabric on chairs in both rooms but vary their floor coverings.

Q *What is the best way to cheer up a small dark room that has few windows, a drab view?*

A Use one light color for walls and curtains (pale blue opens a room the most) and pave the floor with vivid carpeting from wall to wall.

Q *How can I make my living and dining rooms look different and cooler for summer without going in for any major—and costly—changes?*

A Ice your rooms with much white, cool blues and greens—in place mats, flower containers, pillows. Use white china candlesticks instead of silver ones. Remove clutter. Store away the bric-a-brac and bibelots until winter. Put big bunches of greens in your fireplace, a centerpiece of fruit and vegetables or a concoction from your favorite collection—shells, crystal eggs, or whatever—on your dining room table.

Q *When should I paint doors, windows and trim a color that contrasts with the walls?*

A When they are well proportioned and nicely detailed, you might call attention to them with a contrasting color or white. Otherwise, blend them into the background as much as possible by making them the same color as the wall.

Q *Is there any way to use color to improve the proportion of a room that looks too tall?*

A Lower the ceiling visually by adding molding around the walls about a foot from the top, then paint the upper part of the walls and the ceiling a darker color than the walls (not too dark or it will look heavy as a storm cloud).

Q *How can I change my color scheme without changing too much in the room? I don't want to throw out everything and start all over.*

A If your room now has two or more hues, work back to just one color, maintaining the one you like best, adding perhaps an area rug and new slipcovers in that hue. If you have a monochromatic room, introduce a vivid contrast with liberal accents of one or several colors—a piece of painted furniture, a lamp, pillows.

Q *What colors are best with pine paneling?*

A For light pine, try a close harmony of yellows for curtains, rugs, upholstery; for a dark-stained pine, vivid contrasts in rug and fabrics. Here is a good spot for an Oriental.

Q *In a dining room full of wood furniture, how can I relieve the monotonous effect of too much wood and so many smooth surfaces?*

A Rich flow of fabric and pattern adds a lift—a vibrant room-size rug, a brilliant Mexican rebozo across the table, or, over a round top, a colorful cloth that goes down to the floor.

Q *What can I do to make a long, dark hall, with many doors, look lively without taking up its very limited amount of floor space?*

A If the ceiling is high, add color impact there. Or paint each door a different dazzling color. Create a spacious outdoor feeling with white treillage on lettuce green walls. Add cove lighting on long walls or round frost-globes suspended at intervals down the center of the ceiling.

Q *What colors should I use with a fairly typical Oriental rug (mostly reds and blues)?*

A Use the dominant colors of the rug to set the theme; for accents, add a color missing from the rug, such as green. Try light red in a major role on the walls, blue for a sofa, and green for a few bright accents such as small lacquered tables.

PURPLE

A palette of pinky-lilac, *left,* casts a romantic spell over this living-dining room planned by Shelley Mowell. Every hue and nuance are gathered together in the exotic print that covers the Chippendale sofa. Here is the purple that gives such character to the vinyl tile floor, the rosy lavenders, the chalk white of the Art Nouveau lunette above the window and the painted table and dining chairs. Note the importance of the space-stretching mirrored wall, the very contemporary light on a curving stem.

Interplay, not competition, is the moving force in a successful two-color scheme. Each color should be a foil for the other, and both should work together toward the same end. Hues of identical intensity or depth tend to war or merge, and are more difficult to combine successfully than a loud with a muted, a light with a dark. Near relatives—blue and purple, for example—are the safest partners; members of different families—as red and yellow—are the most dynamic. Either way, both should be used in telling strokes, never timidly. If one of the colors is broken up into pattern, its brilliance is reduced, its interest often increased. As a rule, one hue should take precedence, although equal division can be delightful if it is deliberate—and recognizable as such at once. Use that perennial reliable, white, as a background for the colors, or to separate them where you want to, or for accents in strategic places. Depend on black to emphasize, or dark wood finishes to temper over-vitality.

Singing scarlet and humming gold, *left*, the first intense, the second suffused, are an exciting tandem for a study-bedroom. A red wall, quieted down with white dividers, is the center of interest and a lively background for ornaments, pictures, books on glass shelves. Golden rug and bedspread merge into one expanse of sunniness. A built-in desk cantilevered from the bookshelves and a movable file cabinet with pull-out typewriter shelf add up to a compact home office in one corner. The two-color scheme is spelled out once again in leather chairs—one deeply tufted, the other sleek and smooth.

Fresh as clear sea and new grass, *right top*, the clean blue and springtime green in a guest room are preordained by nature to get along superbly. The plaid of blue and white bedspreads is painted on the front of a chest. Duck-covered pillows on wicker chairs bring the rug's green up and away from the floor. Just for the fun of it: yellow and blue needlepoint straps on a luggage rack.

Smashing purple and cool aquamarine, *right below*, play up to each other in a small dining room; there is enough of the lighter color to make its point. Aquamarine lowers the temperature; so does a glass and steel table that also makes the room appear larger. Chest fronts are color steps between purple and red. For relief—a black and white floor, white verticals on one wall. For excitement— a cluster of white hanging fixtures, a marvelous big painting.

GRIGSBY

GRIGSBY

KEENS

YEE

PINTO

Orange and lemon, *above,* a team of luscious colors for the half-and-half cover, transform the big flat surface of a bed into a splash of gaiety. For the rest, texture turns the trick: terry cloth bedspread, rough plaster walls and "headboard," hand-hewn beams above the windows and natural wood matchstick blinds for light control.

Parti-colored amusement, *below,* plus style, are original and easy to achieve when twin beds establish a two-color scheme in a world where beds almost always match! Another split personality: half-blue half-green chair, the sides separated by a length of white frame and striped upholstery. The ample use of white—on the walls, for chest, curtains, rug—calls quick attention to the divided colors in a playful bedroom for a child or guest.

Strong but interlinked contrast, *above,* is achieved by the judicious use of paint and pattern that have blue in common. The vibrant blue of the fireplace wall continues its impact around a library via cornice, dado and window trim. Blue crops up once again in the patterned yellow fabric covering other walls and curtaining the window. Still another way with blue: shiny and tufted on the leather sofa. Tiles, framing the fireplace, freely interpret the fabric design and boldly repeat the two-color scheme.

STOLLER

LEONARD

A lively and varied mingling, *above,* of just two colors
adds spice to the living room of a beach house. A tawny red
and a pale green (muted almost to the color of wet sand) are
used in diverse designs and textures as well as in solid splashes.
The lighter color gives a lift to the architecture—raftered
ceiling, plain-as-can-be door and window, and wall planks where
it is daubed on liberally. The red brightens curved chandelier
arms, flowered curtains and zigzag striped upholstery. A touch to
please a sea captain's personality: the rope accent
around the base of the chaise. Interior design: James Amster.

A room of many colors should be carefully planned but must look spontaneous and uninhibited. Multi-hued excitement is best restricted to a part-time house, room or area. Likely candidates: your weekend hideaway, dining or good-time room, but not a year-round living room unless it is large enough to dominate such exuberance. The colors themselves must be good companions, well matched in strength and character, placed with deliberation, and backed up by expanses of calmness. The only possible accent is black. Before you embark on such an adventurous scheme, face the fact that discipline is essential. Three colors are the easiest to handle; more are a true challenge. They should be close in value and intensity; if all are strong and bright or light and bright, the jump from one to another is gentler on the eye. For orderliness, confine many colors to similar elements such as seat cushions, painted chairs, kitchen cabinets. Or concentrate them in two places, as the rug and a fling of pillows. Tone down the blaze with great sweeps of neutrals—stone, wood, wicker, fur—plus white.

MANY COLORS

FOR INSTANT TAKE OFF

REENS

WARD

Hot and cold color steps, *above,* range from sizzling orange through red- and blue-purples to deep-water blue on seat and back cushions of two sofas that describe a right angle in a contemporary living room. Only the blue is repeated again on a chest against the far wall. Brown leather sofa frames, rich brown wood, washes of white walls, white rug, a white marble tabletop leave the eye free to revel in the parade of colors on the seating group.

A daring dazzle of hues, *left,* is concentrated on cabinet and drawer fronts under white counters and over a white lineup of wall cabinets in a kitchen. The most surprising element here is the confinement of brilliance to well below eye level and well above it. Practical idea: color used as bright clues to the contents of cupboards and drawers.

A giddy palette, *right,* is kept under control by largely limiting it to an array of square pillows and a stretch of striped rug. Audacious additions: scarlet coffee table and undiluted blue seat cushion. All work together to evoke a bang-up holiday mood in the living room of a weekend house. The steadying influence of uninterrupted white, a glass window wall and natural wood ceiling makes the colors behave well. Wicker chairs and the pine frame of the sofa-bed are smaller but essential neutralizers. Note the snap of black used two ways: boldly on a chair frame, in curly spirals on a little table.

GRIGSBY

COLOR POWER
MANY COLORS

Vivid chairs, *above,* become even more so when backed up by neutrals. Identical dining chairs with straw seats take on separate personalities thanks to the simplest means: frames painted three loud colors. One of these —purple with a bite to it—is repeated on a shelf along the wall. This bright board serves two purposes: as a serving table and as sharp underwriting for a group of pictures. More purple: working full-strength or less in the curtains, depending upon whether they are drawn across the window wall or not. Although this dining room seems to glow with color, wood tones really dominate: the red cedar of the clapboard ceiling (fresh idea: clapboards overhead), the deep brown stain on the floor, the light blond of split-bamboo wallpaper and the warm wood of the table.

The punch of a big plaid, *right,* bright and bold as many colors can make it, is backed up by singing yellow-green, a darkly striped rug and a black coffee table. Scarlet and sharp pink pillows, plus a single square of vivid green, give the eye more color pleasure. Space-saving ingenuity in a small room: two sofa-beds end to end along one wall; a hanging light fixture.

South-of-the-border colors,
above, blaze across banks of
kitchen cabinets—exotic sunset warmth
cooled by ample stretches of white
used under, above, and around it.
Here is proof positive that efficiency
loses nothing by wearing a vivid
face. Vertical reaches of uncompromising
orange and yellow contrast with a
wide frontage of pinky-mauve that stops
short above a planning-and-snack
counter and appears again in a row
of simple, spoke-backed chairs. Such
diversified elements as streamlined,
stainless steel cooking units and
refrigerator, a naïve flower picture
that sets the color theme, and a droll
sculpture of a dog, combine without
friction. The true accent: pure black.

WHITE TO QUICKEN OR QUIET

The real wonder of white is its flexibility, its readiness to serve whatever decorative purpose you have in mind. White can tone down a room or wake it up, stay unobtrusively in the background, take the lead or act as an accent. White can work its magic with colors or make its point alone. Back in the 1930s, decorator Syrie Maugham put the all-white room in the limelight. Today white is again a leader, with more practical assets. The new whites—man-made fibers and materials—are easy to clean and keep clean. Team them with some of the classic whites such as cotton, marble, fur. To avoid sterility, ring rich changes with texture and self-patterned weaves. An all-white room can have stunning impact and quicken or quiet the spirits with equal ease.

Besides loving its own company, white brings out the best in every color you put it with: it makes flower shades cleaner and clearer, brash hues easier to take en masse, neutrals warmer and richer. Black, white's opposite, creates the strongest contrast of all. Wood tones of floor and furniture are gentler contrasts. Remember that the play of light and shade does lovely, subtle things to white, giving it an ever-changing, always artful face.

The witchery of white, *left,* complements to perfection a scattering of jewel colors in a light-filled living room. A rainbow of pillows – little splashes of yellow, blue, pink, green – are small in themselves but together conjure up an iridescent magic. Nothing overpowers. Glass-fronted cabinets are painted a pale color; the white sofa is self-effacing. A pair of knowingly scaled coffee tables, two small stools, unmatched open armchairs, tall lamps on yellow cubes, widely spaced paintings, harmonize against white.

GRIGSBY

White plays up a graceful grouping, *above,* in the same room. Ornaments look important on delicate side tables flanking a Louis XV commode; an arrangement of pictures gives height to the whole. For a third dimension (also see foreground, *left*): zebra-striped chairs, chintz-covered table.

The drama of white, *left,* is particularly potent when reinforced by bold blocks of strong color and a few controlled accents of black. In a white dining room, brilliant seat cushions and black paint update standard wicker chairs so they hold their own with a contemporary white table. A bank of chests outlined in black stores the wherewithal for dining. More black: describing squares on the white vinyl-mosaic floor and making sharp statements in pictures and sculpture against the wall. Overhead, two magnets for the eye: a broad reach of scarlet and another of gold tea paper framed by big, structural ceiling beams.

The clean simplicity of white, *right,* becomes still more impressive when played up against black walls in a living room. Inexpensive duck is used for upholstery; dotted white wallpaper covers every inch of the tables. Ornate sconces flanking a silvery mirror carry white up onto the wall. Underfoot: a black and white fur rug retells the theme.

The welcoming warmth of white, *below,* is proved beautifully in the living area of a vacation house. A sofa and several pull-up chairs describe a hospitable circle by the fireplace; the wood frames and a near-bare floor take on extra richness and patina under the influence of flat white. Major contributions to the quality of symmetry here are a pair of white-painted wicker tables and two tall, standing lamps. A glass wall opening onto the patio, which is also furnished in white with bright accents, gives this room a happy look of spaciousness. Two injections of color: a gay picture and a scarlet bench. Two plays of pattern: a fur throw on the sofa and a fur rug on the floor.

GRIGSBY

LYON

To do its job effectively, an accent must contribute a touch or splash of zing to a color scheme. Depending upon a room's dominant colors, you can stir up accent excitement with a vivid hue, a very dark hue (such as navy blue or coffee brown), black or white. Gentle, subtle shades make excellent foils for accents, but cannot be highlights themselves. Generally speaking, brightness flares its sharpest in neutral, white or dark surroundings; strong darks and black are their snappiest when backed up by vivid hues or white. But these are guidelines rather than rigid rules. The one essential: accents should stimulate and vitalize without stridency. They deserve the same clear-eyed consideration as the major colors in a room, and their role should be as carefully planned; indiscriminate accents become a disturbance. You might repeat the same color in strategic places, or shift from plain to pattern, or even add a second kinetic hue, provided you use your highlights deliberately, purposefully—for snap, variation, attention.

GRIGSBY

COLOR ACCENTS

FOR A LIFT

Big blue and green rectangles, *right,* are bold panels from ceiling to floor that enliven a very large living room without overpowering it. The great swacks of color, surrounded by white walls, ceiling and floor, can be seen at one glance but are subtly separated by shallow steps, different levels and distances. The hues themselves evoke summer skies and lawns, as do the leafy plants in troughs along the walls. A quick change from blue and green to red and yellow, for example, could immediately switch the temperature from cool and serene to warm and vibrant. Note that the grouping of pictures on one wall loses none of its impact in spite of the towering color accents.

A touch of bright blue, *left,* steps up a quiet mood in a man's bedroom-library. Calm is created by yards of neutral brown and beige print used on the walls, for curtains and upholstery. The single accent color turns baseboard and ceiling moldings into a frame for the fabric, is repeated in braid on the window valance, and sings again in a wicker armchair at the table-desk. Allover carpeting in off-white makes the room appear larger, as do tall, airy bookcases with glass shelves, brass frames.

A secretary in giddy green, *below,* shakes up the sweet serenity of a pink and white bedroom that might have been too bland without one dollop of daring color. Behind the metal mesh front of the secretary's upper part, a pink interior is proof that this piece of furniture really belongs to the scheme. To create harmony elsewhere, walls and a chaise longue (in the foreground) bloom with matching fabric. A simple device, easily copied: the overhead frame for bed curtain is ceiling molding extended out into the room. Interior design: Blair Catterton.

GRIGSBY

40

SZANIK

COLOR POWER
ACCENTS

Dashing red, *right,* plain and patterned, lifts a near-black and white living room to a highly spirited level. The main seating group centers around a tufted white sofa that merges into the wall behind it, giving full play to the red and white pillows at either end, the red upholstery of furniture at either side. These skillfully placed splashes of one accent color are strong enough to stand up to a vast wealth of fascinating detail—the beamed ceiling, an arrangement of pictures and carvings on the wall, the zebra rug. Dramatic in its simplicity: an uncurtained window with plants beneath it.

Sweet, hot pink, *right below,* flares once on the seat of a green-painted chair and again from the blotter on a desk, thus linking two otherwise unrelated pieces of furniture in a green-drenched living room. A perfect example of the fun that can be had by accentuating the negative is the vivid orange-painted radiator under the tall window.

Two strokes of orange, *far right,* in the form of tole chandeliers, accent the varied palette of subtle neutrals that gives a masculine air to designer David Laurence Roth's kitchen. Dark, walnut-stained cabinets hold the scheme in place. Pattern up the walls and across the ceiling, together with orange fixtures, create great interest overhead.

GRIGSBY

HORST

GRIGSBY

Curving ruby shapes,
below, add up to a pair
of paper chairs and a lamp shade
—the only exuberant color
in a room that is primarily brown
and white. The brown: large,
dark cork tiles on two walls.
The white: shiny paint on almost
everything else including the
herringbone floor and storage
concealing screens. One
of the great advantages of paper
or painted accents is the
fact that you can change them
easily and inexpensively
with the season or your mood.

Vermilion paint, *right,* turns
a very simple table and
two chairs on either side of it
into one collective accent
in a quiet hall. Light taupe
walls, white trim, and a bare
wood floor need the vital
touch of a little strong color.

GRIGSBY

PINTO

A flicker of scarlet, *right,*
is a delightful dividend of
color in an already colorful
little center designed by Michael
Fielding for menu planning
and telephoning. Eked out of a
hall corner, this tiny
room flaunts bright hues—on
the ceiling, walls, floor,
and as vivid lining for the table.

Squares of strong pink,
far right, look as cool as
raspberry sherbet in an orange
and white bedroom. The spacious
corner caters to a woman's
private hours: shelves full of
books, table-desk, chaise
longue, hair dryer, are close
at hand when she needs them.
Interior design: Joseph Braswell.

GOMEL

GRIGSBY

43

NEUTRALS FOR SUBTLETY AND QUALITY

The clue to planning a neutral color scheme can be found in a February landscape laced with snow. All is muted and soft-toned, with no dashes of brilliance except, perhaps, for the scarlet line of a cardinal's flight. The huge span of neutrals runs from near-white through every step of beige and gray to deepest brown and charcoal. Introduce as many as you want into a room without fear of discord. They create a serene mood and a sympathetic setting for Orientals, paintings, furniture of many periods. Make generous use of natural and textured neutrals such as wood, wicker, fur. Add white for background or accents or both. If you want a bit of bite, toss in a spark of sharp color. But give neutrals a prime chance to tell their own story; it has great, quiet style.

MAYA

Gray flannel, *left,* on the walls of a city living room, provides a dark, quiet background for dollops of white and for gleaming surfaces. A French chair is teamed with contemporary cube tables and a canvas wall sculpture in an unexpected but easy relationship. The non-directional design of the rug unites the room's many shapes and patterns (the chair alone has two fabric designs; the quieter one being a plaid cotton on its back). Interior design: David Hicks and Mark Hampton.

Natural materials, *right,* give vigorous personality to the neutral furnishings of this airy, white room in the apartment of designer John F. Saladino. The color spread encompasses several tones, from the near-white of shaggy fur on the sofa to the strong brown of leather on a deeply tufted, floor-low seating unit. In between: a chair's natural wicker, a table's glowing wood, warm pine shutters and mantelpiece. Gray makes its quiet point on the fireplace facing and again in a painting above the mantel, and yet again in the silvery shine of metal lamps. Under all: a near-white rug stretching across most of a dark-stained wood floor.

Exciting shapes, *left,* are silhouetted in deep brown against white. The only vivid splash: three strokes of yellow in a dramatic room where accents must be strong to be effective. Since these one-color shocks are in small areas, a totally different hue (vivid turquoise, for example) can easily be injected instead of yellow for change of pace. This living room, wrested from an old-time carriage house, is vibrant with contrasting forms—graceful spiral staircase, bold sculpture-collage assembled from bits of old millwork, and gleaming metal chairs flanking a deeply cushioned sofa.

Strong patterns, *right,* that contrast dark wood colors with off-white and flax tones, make the beige-to-brown family go bold in a man's bedroom. The loudest pattern is confined to the floor, leaving the rest of the room to a linen wall-covering accented with precise stripes. For a focal point, a dramatic, ceiling-high bed-hanging is fashioned of striped fabric. Interior design: Louis Bromante.

A retiring background, *below,* plays a secondary role in a living room where the limelight rightly goes to sculpture and contemporary paintings. Brown is a subdued color, even when tinged with russet and used to cover two sofas facing each other across the fireplace. The same brown glows gently in small pieces of furniture. Natural wood beams give character to the ceiling without detracting from pictures hung against white walls. In the fireplace: a light "painting."

GOMEL

YEE

HORST

A merger of patterns and fur, *above right,* demonstrates how well the two work together for rich results when all are members of the neutral family. The living room sofa is a layered luxury of texture: suede upholstery overlaid by a brindle-tone fox throw, topped off by leopard velvet pillows. A harmonious pile-up of pattern begins with a geometric design in pale-hued carpeting. On it: a warm-toned flowered rug, and chairs covered in a woven striped fabric. The books establish further pattern interest on the wall.

47

PARIS

COLOR TRICKS AND TREATS

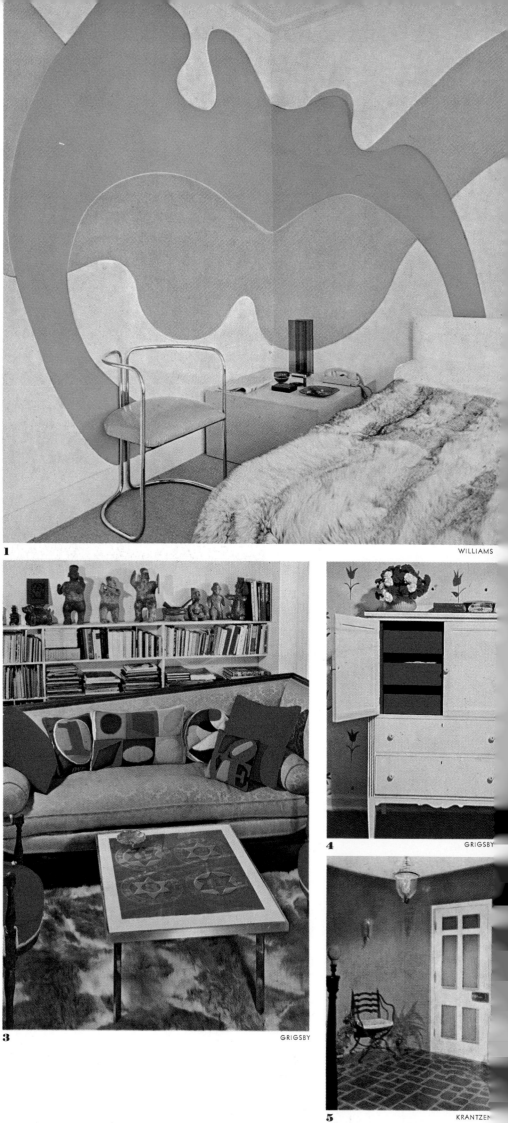

Color is available magic you can buy in cans or by the yard all over this country. There it sits, waiting to be used for just-right touches as well as for entire room schemes. Color can perform a whole bag of conjurer's tricks and sleight-of-hand deception with tremendous ease. It can transform an entire wall or a ceiling cornice into a focal point, can alter perspective, bring distinction to a nondescript floor, even create architectural character where none exists. With a can of paint or a length of fabric, you can wipe out an eyesore, make much of a maverick, or convert a has-been into a sprightly piece of furniture. Exactly what does *your* room need? Gaiety? A little excitement? Amusement? A personal ambiance? Color can provide any or all of these.

Some color happenings are touched off by simply using color in unexpected places or in inventive new ways. Others require more work and skill. But look at everything in your house, from your bathroom fixtures to the beams of your ceiling, as possible candidates for a fresh-hued fling. On these four pages are examples of color's power to persuade, beguile, distract —with magical tricks and rewarding treats.

1   WILLIAMS

4   GRIGSBY

3   GRIGSBY

2   GUERRERO

5   KRANTZEN

6

MASSEY

6

GRIGSBY

6

LEONARD

7

MAYA

9

LYON

1 Waves of color change the shape of a bedroom by abolishing a corner. One's eye concentrates on the movement of orange and blue bands painted across two walls and a door. Self-effacing background and furnishings are white, pale neutrals.

2 Simple and unusual idea: lifting and lightening ceiling beams by painting them sky blue. Blue again on a chair and sofa pillows in this mostly white, cool living room. Interior design: Jaime Parladé.

3 A rigid 19th-century sofa with bolsters at either end becomes wide-awake when decked out with poster-inspired needlepoint pillows. In the same mood: a framed graphic on steel legs makes a color-kindled coffee table.

4 A somewhat dowdy chiffonier is put back in style by painting it white, picking out the reeding on the corner posts with bright red and using more of the same for the interior tray-drawers.

5 Playing up the old-time look of a six-panel front door can be more fun than playing it down. Here, door panels match the green hall walls and are dramatized by white trim and frame. Handsome, practical flooring is slate tile.

6 Colorful revamping: red enamel paint on floor and coffee table; shiny black vinyl on a white chair. Black and white again: in zebra stripes of sofa pillows and needlepoint rug; in a polka-dotted china leopard. Interior design: Russell Norris.

7 Posters are marvelous purveyors of color and gaiety, whether used for a season or for a long time. In designer John Kloss' living room full of neutrals, poster explosion on one wall repeats itself in a mirrored screen by the window.

8 Among the sybaritic pleasures of a sunken tub is its yellow cheerfulness. Molded of reinforced plastic, it has an inner ledge for sitting. Glittering backdrop: eight-foot-high panels of mirror.

9 The red, white and black pattern of two arresting bedspreads inspires a lineup of window shades in a room that uses color sparingly but to great effect, surrounding it with acres of white.

10 A bath-dressing room's too-high ceiling is easily brought down to a reasonable level by painting it a strong mauve-pink and carrying the color a foot or more down the walls. Sprayed to match and serve as an accent: a wicker stool.

1
MASSEY

2
BEADLE

3
MASSEY

4
GRIGSBY

5
KORAB

1 Red serves as a catalyst in the living room of a weekend house. It carpets the floor; it turns two plaids, a check and a poppy-splashed print into amiable companions. Most original performer: a late Victorian chair slicked up with paint and poppies.

2 One vivid hue in two textures wakes up an entrance hall. The mirror and pictures wear velvety fabric-covered frames; the chest wears a coat of shiny lacquer. Black-painted chairs hold down all this exuberance with assurance.

3 Charming, cool, easy to care for: a paisley rug painted on the floor of a summer guest room; the pattern is copied from the bedspread fabric. On two white chairs: striped toweling cushions. At the foot of each bed: striped beach towels. Overhead, natural wood beams support white boards. Interior design: Frank Adams.

4 Red striped and dotted paper gives gay, light appeal to the walls of a bathroom. For straight punch where it will divert but not disturb, the ceiling cornice is painted vivid red. More delicate in feeling: shadow boxes of butterflies hung on the walls.

5 A white guest room in a house outside Santa Fe boasts no architectural distinction but its heavily beamed ceiling. Furniture is sparse and simple; curtains, bedspread and slipcover are plain white cotton. But the room is set ablaze and made quite unique by merely painting the board floor.

6 Bouquets on a white fabric bring a scattering of color to a white bedroom, and also inspire two important concentrations of color: over-scaled flowers in one corner of the rug; a chest and mirror in green from the print. Interior design: Edward M. Benesch.

7 Bold bands of color march across the floor and straight up one wall of a small boy's bedroom. The floor is vinyl, laid in stripes; the wall is wood-paneled with fold-back window shutters. Storage units are demountable. Interior design: Mallory-Tillis.

8 A rich brown wall is the quiet backdrop for a glittering "composition" of eighty Christmas tree balls kept tidily in their packing containers and framed. Brown pillow covers match the wall behind them and take a back seat to give an eye-compelling quilt the attention it deserves.

LEONARD

6

7

GRIGSBY

8

PINTO

RED, WHITE AND BLUE TRENCHANT AND TIMELESS

Red, white and blue is the fascinating trio that occurs and recurs from time to time in both fashion and interior design. It is a very special trio, combining verve and sparkle with historical significance. It not only represents the flag colors of the United States, Great Britain and France, but of twenty-one other countries as well.

Twice in the last hundred years, this heady trio has put Liberty in fashion. In the early 19th century, the French wore navy blue coats, white trousers and regimental red ribbons, white dresses with red and blue scarves, and, in harmony with the trend, put red and blue in their white neoclassical drawing rooms. The second time, in the United States, from 1940 to 1943, the American flag flew in fashion, with blue coats trimmed in red, worn with white pancake berets. In the country, hostesses spread out milk glass to blaze against blue linens and created centerpieces of red carnations or tulips or geraniums. A great wave of wallpaper striped with red and white and blue and white swept into interior design, and the shiny red door that will last forever was first seen.

Red and white was opulent when the Edwardians introduced it into their parlors. In the twenties, Elsie de Wolfe who, along with Syrie Maugham, created the all-white look, added a red carpet and red and blue chintz to a white room to make decorating news.

And now, again, we are living in a period of red, white and blue. This time it has nothing to do with chauvinism. After psychodelia, it is not only virile but has its own aptitude for looking sparkling new. Dark blue walls have an excitement of their own. Red fabric flows against them and white furniture looks appetizing. Everywhere you look you can put your hands on these colors. And wherever your eye asks for red, white and blue, you may have this classic combination.

The snap of flag colors, *below,* in a needlepoint rug from Portugal, sets up the tricolor theme for a study. The lounge chair's cerulean hue makes a visual link between the rug's deeper blue and the antique French screen. For balance: much off-white swathed across walls and windows, with the tricolor repeated in moldings which border the ceiling and frame the curtains. Interior design: Charles Dear.

The bravura of blue, *right,* updates the old-fashioned high-ceilinged living room of designer Ronald Ferri. The walls' heavy trim all but disappears into the blue, as does the matching sofa. A switch from the usual way of playing bright colors against white, the blue expanse intensifies the whiteness of the sculpture and the gleam of an Italian lamp. The well-worn parquet floor is snapped out of its retiring role by a coat of white paint, plus a zebra rug with red edging—a beautiful hoax since it too is done with paint. Fun also: an eye-riveting red table cut from a carton.

GRIGSBY

Airy patterns, *above,* each with a fresh outdoor feeling, create an effect that is surprisingly dainty for the usually bold red-white-blue combo. Two over-scaled designs—the cane of the rug and the flowers on a chair and pillows—are kept in bounds while a delicate paper is given a field day. It covers all walls to make a sprightly background for simple furnishings. A pin-dotted fabric was quilted for spreads.

Flamboyant design, *right,* of feather-swirled paper on ceiling and walls, brings tricolor excitement to the small confines of a guest closet.

Crisp stripes, *above,* in chintz curtains and walls, help make a little boy's room look neat—a feat abetted by the fact that toys generally come in primary colors, making just-right accents for a red, white and blue scheme. Interior design: Burt Wayne.

Equal amounts of red and blue, *above,* in upholstery checks, team up with blue and white ticking in a country living room. Ticking covers the whole window wall, makes valances and curtains, and also adds its simple charms to an antique chair.

Red and blue, back to back, *left,* come on strong in a reversible bonded jersey that is cleverly used for a tailored canopy and bedspread. The wide-awake red quickly makes the bed the focal point of the room; at night, the deep blue seen from the pillows soothes the eye. Emphasizing the richness of the colors are intriguing textures, including those of the wool jersey chairs, felt pillows, and suede cloth wall covering. Here, white, added sparingly, but in rousing hard-line patterns, brings out all the razzle-dazzle possible in a red, white and blue scheme. Interior design: Renny Saltzman.

YEE

COLOR POWER
RED, WHITE AND BLUE

Tricolor wallpaper, *left,* on a peaked ceiling, leads
the eye upward and visually expands an attic
room for two boys. Nearer eye level, matching fabric
covers bunks and makes a window shade. White walls, a
screen that repeats red, white and blue in broad
strokes, and a red floor, keep the scene under control.

GUERRERO

Friendly bistro mood, *above,* is evoked with a
checkered cloth and red-painted bentwood chairs in
a kitchen. Blue, Moorish-style, vinyl tiles pave
the floor and face the cabinet under a deep blue sink.

The look of today, *left,* in an otherwise traditional
dining room, is created largely by unconventional
ways with color. Brilliant red on chairs and a corner
cabinet vividly accents an equally brilliant blue.
The blueberry color is everywhere, even inside
the Chippendale breakfront which is painted to show off a
family collection of treasured old china. White goes
two ways in this room: by itself on walls and ceiling,
it exerts a calming influence; in the carpet, it brightens
the blue to make the room's one electrifying
pattern. Interior design: Stephen Mallory of Mallory-Tillis.

GRIGSBY

Chapter 2

BACKGROUNDS

THE ELEMENTS THAT MAKE A ROOM

A room's background consists of the various elements that wrap it up into its particular shape, together with the fixed openings which punctuate that shape. Walls, windows, ceiling, floor and, in some cases, a fireplace are the prime factors. Lucky indeed is the person who can have a voice in creating or controlling the structural beginnings of her room's background. Most of us make the best of various enclosures whose size, shape, exposure, surface materials and window placement are established and cannot be changed without extensive remodeling. Therefore, the challenge is to figure out a room's built-in assets and liabilities together with any relatively simple changes or additions that will be worth the trouble involved, plus every device that can counteract the liabilities which must remain. These calculations are imperative because structural backgrounds are really the framework, whether lean and lovely or uneven and in need of camouflage, upon which you construct decorative effects.

Probably the one element in a room that can be your staunchest ally or most severe handicap is proportion. It is the simple truth that a beautifully proportioned room can really do no wrong. It may be low-ceilinged and intimate or lofty and elegant; size is not the controlling factor. Proportion is a matter of relationship—between length, width and height, between walls and windows, doors and other openings. A badly proportioned room is awkward, graceless, lacking in assurance. It needs all the help it can get: a clever use of color, materials, furnishings, pictures and other distractions to draw attention away from poor shaping.

What you do with a room's background is enormously important because the areas involved are so big (walls, ceiling and floor) or so conspicuous (windows and fireplace). A sound and simple beginning is to concentrate on whatever good elements the room already possesses. For example, if it is fortunate enough to have a stone or mellow brick wall, play up the outdoor color and outside texture of the natural material. Get all the attention value you can from a dramatic window wall, handsome fireplace or high, peaked ceiling. If trim is lovely, give it prominence. If a floor is beautiful, count yourself lucky. If not, decide how best to put the sizable area underfoot to work for the entire room's benefit.

The following pages are a rich mine of creative ideas for making the most of a room's background: ingenious inventions for walls, windows, ceilings and floors, and imaginative structural elements to stir your imagination if you plan to build or remodel your house.

Brick, stone and paint, *right,* are three good reasons why the walls of this living room dominate its other basic elements. Strong contrast: the variegated brick wall, the rough stone surface beyond it, and the eggplant color of a picture wall. Off-white ceiling and mushroom-toned rug take a quiet back seat. The simple fireplace establishes a natural focal point for a seating group. Interior design: David Whitcomb.

GRIGSBY

WALLS

HOW TO SET THE SCENE WITH THEM

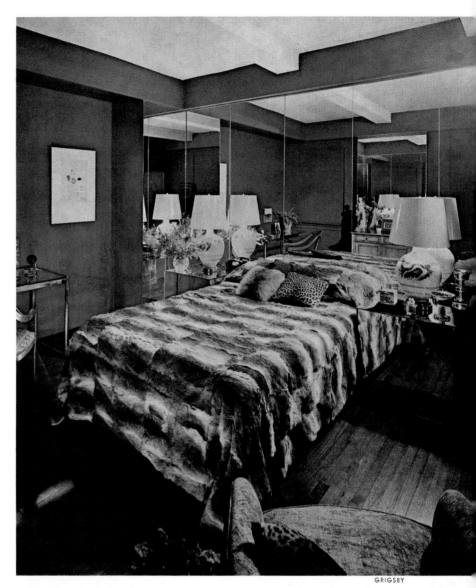

GRIGSBY

Walls enclose space; they establish a room's dimensions and essential shape. They surround you on all sides, and you are very much aware of them or not, depending on how they are treated. Painted a self-effacing color and used as a background for paintings, bookshelves, ornaments or exciting lighting, walls themselves become unimportant. But cover them with noticeable color or pattern, spotlight one or more with handsome, natural surfacing, a dominant hue or splashy design, and you create a magnet for the eye, a positive statement.

Although walls add up to the largest area in a room, they have a great talent for optical illusion. You can reduce their apparent height by stopping them short at top or bottom—extend the ceiling down onto them, or simulate a dado painted to match the trim, and start the wall color or covering above the dado. (In either case, use molding to define the break.) It is easy to minimize irregularities in walls by using a color or covering bold enough to steal the limelight. If you want a feeling of spaciousness, you can achieve it with a mirrored wall or a coat of paint in a light, clear color. (Sky blue is one of the best.) You can even alter the shape of a room by "moving" a wall; advance it with a strong, bright hue; push it back with a pale, subdued tone.

For a sense of unity, repeat your wall's color or pattern out in the room. For high-flying drama, do the opposite; play up a vibrant wall color by limiting it to walls alone, teaming it with neutral furnishings.

Wall coverings range from tiles to brick, stone, wood and mirror, from rough to shiny texture, from fabric to paper and paint. Here is power a-plenty to make your walls perform cleverly in a starring or supporting role.

Armfuls of flowers, *left,* strewn across yards of cotton— inexpensive enough to buy by the bolt without breaking the bank— bring delicious freshness and gaiety to the living room of a tiny 1890 house. The wall pattern comes right into the room on a trio of white-painted chairs. (Most of the furniture was once part of an Edwardian "suite" which, when lacquered and treated to a pretty print, starts life anew.) Played against the flowering are two geometrics, one in an Irish rug of crocheted linen, the other on half-round tables flanking the fireplace with its carved motto, "Vanity of vanities; all is vanity." Note the device for lowering the ceiling: its off-white tone continues down the wall to a simple molding. Interior design: Eleanor Ford.

Explosive color and mirror, *above,* on the walls of a man's small bedroom, give it both dramatic impact and an illusion of spaciousness. The brilliant blue, real and reflected, fills the room with deep vibrancy almost to saturation, and establishes a very masculine mood. The strong hue and silver-gleaming glass are countered with quiet neutrals, ranging from the wood tones of a bare, sable-stained floor to the variegated browns and off-whites of a soft, luxurious bed cover. Accents are stark white—for lamp shades and the mat of a picture.

Split-color tiles, *below,* pulse across a bathroom's walls and shower stall. The design is a clever composition using one glazed tile pattern—a square divided diagonally—repeated in an almost nonstop pattern of diamonds alternating with zigzag rows. For extra flair, towel holders are mounted on bas-relief cherub tiles; their presence quickly pointed out by a sharp yellow for towels. The other background elements—beamed ceiling, stone-paved floor, carved and green-stained door—are also dramatic in design but play secondary roles because they are dominated by the patterned walls.

Brown velvet paper, *right,* on the walls and right across the ceiling, makes a master bedroom as snug as a deep, quiet cave. The dark walls also prove to be a marvelous background for part of an extensive art collection, as witness the three pictures on the wall behind a big bed covered in a white texture. Interior design: William Baldwin.

GRIGSBY

BEADLE

Bamboo fretwork, *below,* on walls covered with a pale patterned cotton, quickly establishes a pervasive Oriental feeling in a reading, entertaining and dining room. Pale naturals on all background areas (floor and ceiling as well as walls) bring unity to the multi-purpose room. For added liveliness, two different fabric designs are alternated—the Chinese-inspired cotton on walls, banquette base and a few pillows; a white and metallic gold-flowered cotton on ceiling and banquette cushions. For sharp accents: a lacquer screen and small red pillows in the same flowered pattern as the cushions.

Rough stained boards, *below,* on a living room's walls, flatter by contrast a glittering gamut of antiques and opulent fabrics. A far cry from the brocade-and-pilaster backgrounds, formerly associated with fine 18th-century furniture, the rugged country-textured wood is stained a deep blue, with undertones of the wood itself. Ceiling beams, valances and curtains carry the blue overhead and across the windows. Interior design: John FitzGibbons.

GRIGSBY

GRIGSBY

PINTO

HILL

PINTO

Heavily textured plaster, *above,* coats the walls in a room where everything is the better for being simple in both materials and design. Nothing requires finicky care. Against one wall, books are shelved in a row of white-painted boxes. With only a sheet of plywood and a jigsaw, architect Jean-Claude Martin made his dining table—its base fashioned of pieces left over after he cut out the top.

Old bricks, *left,* give a living room wall softly variegated coloring and wonderful texture. Both are played up during the day by light pouring down from a huge skylight. Mellow heirloom furniture, a traditional pattern covering the sofa and a contemporary painting above it are linked harmoniously by the ageless brick background. Interior design: Rosa Miller.

BAER

Local stone, *above,* was used for a massive, free-standing fireplace in a glass-walled, vacation pavilion. Unique feature: two angled side wings or short walls of stone on either side of the wide chimney breast. They evoke a sense of snugness around the hearth and subtly partition the huge room.

Glowing pine planks, *left,* on an attic's end wall, bring warmth, height and importance into a stepchild area. Curtaining of mattress ticking—also a vertical pattern—makes a wall along one side where it was needed to conceal storage space salvaged from the head-bumping area under the eaves. Pretending that structural beams and mid-room supports like these can be ignored is foolhardy; treating them as if they were part of a giant sculpture adds immense pow inexpensively.

Cedar shakes, *right,* shingle a living room wall in a summer retreat by the ocean. The shingles, used also on the exterior of the house, neatly unite indoors and out, as do fabrics which share a common motif of fern patterns, cool as a forest dell. A rug woven to simulate random-width, pegged planking partly covers oak flooring that has been bleached to the color of sunlit sand. Architects: Gifford & Fuller. Interior design: Yale Burge.

MAYA

WINDOWS

**HOW TO CONTROL
THEIR
ROLE IN A ROOM**

Windows are attention-getters, and how could it be otherwise? Whether they are carved out of solid walls or are actually entire walls themselves, their transparency sets them apart. So does their position, confronting you head on, and most often at eye level when you turn in their direction. In the daytime, windows are conspicuous as the source of light. At night, depending upon whether they are covered or not, they turn into expanses of curtains, shades, blinds or glittering darkness.

You can achieve almost any result you want with window treatments: bring the outdoors indoors or create a cozy ambiance; temper light and sound; play up a beautiful view or efface a tiresome one; even hide horrors such as blank walls and fire escapes. You can make your windows as provocative as paintings or tone them down to background quietness. Consider the *play* of light as well as the *control* of light. Use the first to establish a mood, the second to cater to your comfort. You can do a great job of both with the many devices available now: blinds of all kinds, louvered shutters, various screenings, coarsely or fine woven translucent fabric. You can use shades that pull up or down; either way, their flatness increases the apparent size of a room and emphasizes its architectural quality. Curtains can camouflage as well as decorate, make a window appear smaller or larger, give the illusion of a window wall, bracket two windows into one. Valances can add or subtract inches of height at a window, depending upon whether they are hung high or low. You can use combinations such as curtains with shades, blinds or shutters, for more interest and efficiency, but avoid fussiness. A simple treatment is always the best.

GRIGSBY

Double tiebacks, *above*, holding aside yellow overcurtains of heavy cotton moiré, let more light into a library. The wall-matching curtains are simply looped over a fabric-covered rod set within the window frame. Sheer curtains are the same shade of white as the molding.

Swing-out curtains, *right*, on movable brackets, allow an unobstructed view of a pretty garden along one side of a dining room in a beautifully restored 1857 house. White woodwork around the windows—painted to play up their classic beauty—also does much to set off the dramatic parade of fabric, and calls attention, too, to all the green outside.

A paisley frame, *left*, of sailcloth in sunshine colors, softens the aspect of sliding glass doors in a poolside party room. The paisley overcurtains, permanently tied back, serve as daytime shields for sheer white curtains that are drawn across the glass at night. The shape of the valances, which are lined in yellow, is repeated in the all-yellow valance at the outer edge of the porch roof. Interior design: Jamie Ballard.

ECKERT

GRIGSBY

65

GRIGSBY 1

BACKGROUNDS WINDOWS: CURTAINS

1 To spark interest in a long, narrow hall, each huge window is flanked by flowered curtains, their design a bright stand-in for the garden outlook whenever the curtains are closed. Linking the many panels into a united whole is a matching strip of fabric applied to the wall above them.

2 Solving the problems of a window wall as troublesome as they come (this one has a sill-high radiator, a dismal view and a clutter of window-side pipes) takes the combined forces of shoji screens and permanently drawn curtains. The curtaining, a semi-opaque fiber glass with a pretty Persian motif, filters the light and is not affected by steam heat behind it. Interior design: Manashaw & Daggett.

3 For a simple way to carry a bedroom's one-and-only print to the window area without rivaling the majesty of the ceiling-high fabric headboard, curtains of the same damask are only three-quarter length and hung low. Their headings are the same harlequin points as those on the canopy and coverlet. Used above these curtains—to cut down morning light—is more of the same sheer fabric that frames the headboard.

4 To step up a window niche's old-fashioned charms and soften its long reach from ceiling to floor, curtains are made of theatrical gauze and fringed with tassels. As allies of the architecture, the panels are hung within the window molding and are similar in color. Interior design: Barton L. Davis.

5 To offset the lowness of the ceiling in a large living room made from two parlors in a remodeled farmhouse, two ruses are employed: the valances are the narrowest of rolls set as high as possible; and curtains of the same moiré-patterned fabric spill down onto the floor. Interior design: Peter Prince.

6 For sheer beauty and grace, windows of a Palm Beach room overlooking a lovely court are framed by cloud-light curtains of sari cloth, handwoven of silk and gold thread. To take advantage of the view, the matching valance is set above the window panes. Interior design: Clare J. Hoffman.

7 For a unifying effect at corner windows, paper and matching fabric go on a delightful binge together; the wallpaper taking over wherever the fabric ends. The combination of café curtains below, Roman shades and valances above, allows flexible control of air, light, privacy and the view.

LEONARD 2

3

GRIGSBY

LYON

4

GRIGSBY

5

GRIGSBY

6

GRIGSBY

7

CURTAINS AND SHADES

One persuasive color, *right, top,* for a window bay's taffeta curtains and silk moiré shades, blends the bay with the room. So do these pretty and clever ways of handling the curve: the curtains' balloon puffing, delightful for its own sake, is made full enough to cover up the separation between the shades; and the valance's scallops are deeply slashed to round the gentle bow gracefully. Interior design: Angelo Donghia of Burge-Donghia.

Two tangy partners, *right, center,* a shade and curtains of a print that echoes the tangerine burlap on walls of a study, redeem one awkwardly placed window. The same print covers two armchairs. For zing: a stinging yellow used unabashedly on the largest piece of upholstered furniture. Interior design: Angelo Donghia.

Three powerful plays, *right, bottom,* with one print—in sill-length curtains, in shades, in cushions topping radiator enclosures—create drama out of slim pickings: two small windows and unsightly radiators. Neat detail: rolls covered with matching fabric for the window headings. The print also sets the room's color scheme, the blue going to the floor in the rug's sharp border. Interior design: Burt Wayne.

Four refreshing choices, *left* and *above,* among shades and curtains, quick-change a room for a party, a season. The shades, always in place, are unnoticeable when not in use; the curtains form part of the room's permanent background of quiet whites. Abetting the switches in mood: changeable accents, including roll-down wall panels. A Mexican cotton shade, *left,* brings on festive winter reds. Orange stripes, *above, top,* evoke a crisp autumn mood. Embroidered linen shades, *above, center,* say springtime. Curtains alone, *above,* are cool for summer. Interior design: Jack Lenor Larsen.

GRIGSBY

BEADLE

BACKGROUNDS
WINDOWS: SHADES

GRIGSBY

YEE

Awning stripes, *far left,* on a Roman shade, add a sunshine color at the window of a study where bookshelves would crowd floor-length curtains. Also, the simple window treatment is a nice foil for the lively pattern of books. To let in daylight, the shade folds up into accordion pleats. Interior design: David Eugene Bell.

A shaft of chintz, *left, center,* to match the covering of the sofa, takes over at night to shade a ceiling-high slot of a window which was added to a game room to bring more daylight into a dark corner. Interior design: Melvin Dwork.

The silvery shimmer, *far left, bottom,* of Mylar vinyl shades adds the snap of today to a living room in an old-time apartment building. To camouflage the room's uneven soffits and the unmatched bookcases flanking the two windows, striped curtains are hung inside the room. And for more shimmer and snap, they are hung from a chrome shower rod and rings.

Two-way control, *left, bottom,* of shades that go up from the floor and down from the top of a window wall, provides a highly flexible means of adjusting the light and the view and insuring privacy. In antique gold, the shades make a nice transition from outdoor colors to vivid indoor hues. The dark verticals of the frames are carried into and across the room by the specially designed flooring. Interior design: Paul Krauss.

Light-filtering wool, *right,* in handwoven shades, keeps the strongest sunlight from pouring into an airy garden room. Curtains for so many windows would have muffled the room in fabric and banished the garden atmosphere. Semitranslucent, the shades provide individual sun control for each window and the garden door, too. The off-white coloring merges with the room's cool theme and the simplicity of the furnishings. Interior design: Michael Taylor.

GRIGSBY

WILLIAMS

GRIGSBY

Narrow aluminum slats, *far left,* rev up the old Venetian blind concept in a remodeled kitchen where sleekness counts. (In this working area, so do privacy and light control since the room faces onto a city sidewalk—a situation in which blinds are at their best.) The blind's sleek look is abetted by barely visible braided cords instead of more conventional fabric tapes. On each side of the center window, old-fashioned tinted panels subdue slivers of the busy scene yet let in a fair share of light. Interior design: Angelo Donghia of Burge-Donghia.

A glass "construction," *left,* by Michael Haynes, in front of windows at one end of a living room, turns daylight into vivid kaleidoscope patterns as it comes into the room. Glimpses of the garden can be seen through the design. On adjacent walls, paintings by outstanding contemporary artists are well lighted from the ceiling.

Vertical linen strips, *left, bottom,* which can be adjusted to control light, pull across the windows in a living room where horizontal slats would make the ceiling seem too low. The slats' fabric makeup fits into the scheme of neutrals, from creamy beige to dark brown, varied by many materials and rich textures. Interior design: Burt Wayne.

Folding panels, *right, top,* that frame insets of the same flowered fabric which is on the beds, make a pretty, easy-to-manage stand-in for curtains across tall windows and glass doors. When closed, the panels are anti-sunlight, pro-privacy strokes of pattern; open, the panels let the glass bring the fringing woods practically into the room. Interior design: Robert Wedel.

Pierced screening, *right,* of Moroccan cut redwood, filters sunlight streaming into a bedroom of a Palm Beach house without totally eclipsing the ocean view. When the sun is indirect, the panels can be pushed to each side, one behind the other. Interior design: Falasco & Smith.

Louvered shutters, *far right,* the same off-white as the walls, adjust to bring the outdoors in and also help keep things simple in a game room stripped down for summer to its most carefree cool: the wicker, steel and glass furniture is airy; the hanging garden breezy; and the ceramic tile floor bare and uncluttered.

STOLLER

GRIGSBY

BACKGROUNDS
WINDOWS:
SIX WAYS TO REGULATE LIGHT

BEADLE

CEILINGS

**HOW TO
LIFT,
LOWER
AND
ADORN
THEM**

A ceiling establishes a room's height. And all but the most standard heights affect us emotionally. A soaring ceiling in a big room has exciting impact; in a small room it may be depressing. A truly low ceiling has informal charm for many, but it tends to make others—notably tall people—feel cramped. You can fool the eye quite easily, however, with color. Ceilings appear higher if they are lighter in tone than walls, and seem lower if they are darker.

With many materials to choose from, you can make a ceiling as decorative as other elements in a room (and in a long room where your every glance is apt to include part of the ceiling, this becomes most important). A patterned wallpaper or fabric that carries out the room's theme can be dramatic overhead. Choose a geometric or any other design with no direction, so the pattern looks right from any part of the room. Stripes should meet at a central point. For texture, consider caning, matting, treillage— or emphasize such structural elements as exposed rafters, beams.

Brilliant color, *right,* on the ceiling, needled by the white of painted beams, adds great dash to a dining room where walls are kept simple to serve as background for a fascinating array of drawings and prints. The glowing red is also a color link to nearby rooms: the same bright hue lines the entrance hall and covers sofas in the living room. At beam height and just below, lighting was built in to illuminate the prints and cast a soft glow on the curtained wall. Underfoot: a mass of pattern that balances the room's mass of strong color overhead.

Wooden egg crates, *left,* all over the ceiling, add texture, pattern and a good measure of acoustical control in a room that has the uncluttered calm of a Japanese setting. An openwork ceiling of this kind provides another advantage: lighting can be placed above it in strategic places, thus eliminating the need for many floor and table lamps.

A Bukhara rug, *below, left,* warm in color, lively in design, hangs by chains from the ceiling to achieve a highly dramatic effect— no small feat in a room eclectically furnished. Among the many riches: early Coptic weaves framed in clear glass against a blue felt wall.

Woven willow, *below,* between narrow rafters of a sloping ceiling, gives the living room in a beach house the cool rustic air of a thatched house. The effect is enhanced by a shelf of plants high on the wall at one end of the room. In the same holiday mood: the mix of Mexican, Spanish, Portuguese furnishings. Interior design: Michael Taylor.

PINTO

GRIGSBY

LYON

REENS

74

KORAB

A massive vault, *left,* of bricks, an architectural achievement of great splendor, creates high drama and provides a wonderfully warm and commodious background for entertaining. The ceiling, called a bóveda, is the work of skilled Mexican masons (to fashion the vault's contour, the mason follows the curve of his hat brim). Crowning touch: a cupola to invite a stream of light. Architects: O'Neil Ford & Associates.

Bold beams and skylights, *above,* an unusual combination, interact beautifully in this long, low room: the beams, like wave upon wave, counteract the room's narrowness, and their massive simplicity is a good match for the room's large furniture and natural materials (floor, hassocks and sofa base are all of adobe); the two skylights keep those areas of the room that are not near the window from being a gloomy cavern.

A striped tent, *below, left,* is a decorative notion that first became popular when Napoleon went campaigning (his own study at Malmaison was decorated this way). Like so many good ideas, it seems ever fresh, combining tailored crispness with a romantic quality. The tent lining this square room is of wallpaper. Strips were cut to make the ceiling "seams," and a cornice was added to break the long march of stripes.

A gay treillage, *below,* is created by a fresh-as-spring checkered paper across a slightly peaked ceiling. Swagged cornices and arched window frames of the same paper complete the effect of sheltering the garden of oversized flowers on the bedspread and slipcover. The white walls and pale carpet are muted accompaniment for the counterpoint of checks and flowers. The color scheme evokes a cool, summer day. Interior design: James Childs Morse.

LEONARD

LEONARD

FLOORS
HOW TO SUIT THEM TO YOUR NEEDS

Floors anchor your room. A wood floor stained a dark tone that still allows the grain to show, then waxed and polished to perfection, creates a rich, neutral background. Use a light-toned finish for an airier look or to extend the light sweep of a pale-colored rug. For gaiety that is inexpensive, paint a soft wood floor a solid color (an unexpected hue has the most impact). Or try your hand at a simple geometric or stenciled pattern. Or copy 18th-century country craftsmen who painted naïve versions of black and white marble squares so amateurish that they fooled no one!

Floors of other natural materials such as stone, brick or terrazzo are especially suited to foyers and rooms where large expanses of glass seem to bring the outdoors inside. (For warmth and quiet, place area rugs in strategic places.) Man-made hard floor coverings range from glazed tiles to various compositions such as vinyl. Depending on the overall effect you want, use such coverings plain or patterned.

Flooring can vary from one room to another but the break should be defined by a lintel, steps or other means. When maintenance is a problem, use practical floor coverings that are neutral in value, with a smallish design. Solid, light or dark colors show soil easily.

White ceramic tiles, *left,* pave the living room of a New York brownstone, bringing lightness and sparkle to a room that has no windows on the long walls. The curved geometric pattern of the tiles also helps offset the rectilinear quality of the rest of the room. For still more light reflection—all the better for viewing the room's treasure of sculpture, paintings and collage—the walls, too, are white. For a feeling of added spaciousness, every ceiling in the house is sky blue.

A parquet floor, *below,* of warm wood tones in a simple pattern, has a wonderful unifying effect on a room filled with diverse furnishings. Another unifying element: the neutral color scheme. And still another: the fabric border skirting the white slipcovers; the woven design neatly restates both the darkest tone of the floor and the verve of its rich grains.

Brick-patterned tiles, *far left*, of vinyl—three "bricks" to a tile—make a sturdy and practical base for the kitchen of an old San Francisco house. The floor's design of tiles, laid in alternating directions, complements the cane-patterned wall covering which masks the room's old jigs and jogs. Interior design: Eleanor Ford.

Painted checkerboard, *left*, a just-for-fun design spread across the wood floor of a country dining room, adds immense flair, largely because the bold harlequin pattern is so unexpected a contrast with the opulent Chinese screen across one wall. Bamboo, black as the floor's dark squares, frames the wall screen and extends around the whole room as moldings. Interior design: Mrs. Burrall Hoffman.

Flowered fabric, *bottom, far left*, in an 18th-century pattern, makes a novel, delightful flooring for a boldly modern dining room. The fabric has been laminated to clear vinyl and cut into 22-inch tiles, then separated by narrow strips of black vinyl. The underfoot expanse of black and white makes the room look larger.

Waxed brick, *bottom, left*, is the perfect flooring for a country living room used for dining and pot gardening, too. The bricks add warm color and texture, take much wear and tear. Imaginative idea: the backdrop for the hanging garden is composed of four panels from an old-fashioned elevator cage. Interior design: William Cecil.

Slate slabs, *right*, were the original flooring of this one-time porch when it was open to the elements. After the porch was enclosed, the floor was simply sanded smooth and then waxed. Glowing and handsome, the stone makes a cool background for an airy living area during hot weather, and can be warmed up with a rug to offset winter's cold. Interior design: David Barrett.

BEADLE

Ceramic tile, *above*, in a four-part repeat pattern, gives a small garden room a Mediterranean look and an easy-to-clean floor. The glazed tiles have a built-in abrasive to help prevent slipping.

GUERRERO

GUERRERO

Brick pattern, *left,* that is agreeable from any angle, in a vinyl which is easy to care for, makes a highly practical floor covering for a home workroom catering to a variety of pursuits (this one is studio, game room and airy guest room). Interior design: Melanie Kahane.

LEONARD

Twisted strands, *above,* simulated in vinyl that reproduces the texture and pattern of antique rope carpeting, make a happy, easy-to-maintain choice for the hall floor of a beach house. The spiral staircase, its design as intriguing as a giant piece of sculpture, leads to a sea view. Interior design: James Amster.

Grand slam design, *left,* made from a vinyl floor covering that comes by the roll, gives character and depth to a dining room. Three different colorings of the stone-chip pattern were used to create the big composition, one that would not be feasible with small tiles. The idea can readily be adapted to a room of any size. (The curves are easily plotted with a beam compass, using the corners of the room as the pivot points).

Irregular slabs, *right,* of darkest slate filled with near-white grout, set up a stimulating mood for dining. The floor is the only strong pattern in a room where other surfaces—the Philippine mahogany paneling, natural leather chairs, polished marble and steel table—are comparatively bland neutrals. Interior design: Emily Malino.

BEADLE

You can put interest underfoot in various ways, but carpeting and rugs are the most sensuous: soft to the step, quiet to the ear. Use wall-to-wall carpeting or a room-size rug to expand apparent dimensions with their broad sweeps. Small-scale geometric patterns and muted designs, such as those in many Orientals, are very adaptable. They are a wise choice for dining rooms and much-used areas because they do not readily show spots. Strong pattern is most dramatic but requires the balance of other strengths—large-scale furniture, plenty of vivid or dark upholstery—to keep the rug down on the floor.

Use area rugs to define parts of a room such as dining and living areas, or to change proportions such as the stretch of a too-long room. Use them to hold furniture groupings together or for splashes of interest on a neutral or hard floor.

For rich, natural texture, you can't beat fur rugs. Many of them come in wonderful shapes, arresting patterns. Above all, they are luxurious and equally suited to country or urban rooms.

Dare to mix different kinds of rugs, either in separate areas of a room, or by putting a small decorative rug on a large plain carpet.

Stair and hall carpeting may be bold or retiring, depending on whether you wish it to attract attention away from uninteresting surroundings. When continued from one level to another, stair carpeting can be a superb catalyst.

RUGS AND CARPETS

HOW TO CHOOSE AND USE THEM

LEONARD

A fabulous Oriental, *above,* is both the inspiration and the catalyst for a dramatic scheme of brilliant solid colors and splashes of white against dark-painted walls. Too beautiful to cover, the Oriental also inspires an unconventional arrangement of furniture that allows the important design elements to be seen without interruption. Worth noting: the upholstered pieces have no rug-hiding skirts. Interior design: John FitzGibbons.

MASSEY

A sharp geometric, *above,* non-directional in design, easily climbs steps—these from a quiet library to an equally quiet, raised alcove for sleeping. The wall-to-wall carpeting keeps the room's main pattern—and virtually its only relief from hushing gray—below eye level where it won't shake up the drowsy. Conducive to sleep: the flannel, velvety and quiet as a mouse, that covers ceiling, walls and bed. Interior design: Alberto Pinto.

An exuberant design, *left,* in a rug from France, spreads its powers across a collector's library—and its powers have to be considerable in a room filled to the brim with myriad shapes and patterns (only the ceiling is left serenely untouched). Among the rug's strengths: the singing red ground; the orderly repeat of its formal motif; the defining strips of sharp yellow. Marvelous background for all the treasures: placating green walls, just a shade darker than the greens in the rug.

85

Several small Oriental rugs, *below,* in many muted patterns, give mellow interest to a huge expanse of flooring in the raftered living room of a remodeled 300-year-old barn. The rugs are skillfully placed to form yet another pattern on the beautifully grained and glowing wood. The spacious, 19-foot-high room is also capable host to enormous variety from other sources—bricks, chintz, books—and to a mix of early American antiques, deep-seated upholstered chairs and sofa, diverse decorative objects.

Two unrelated weaves, *right,* define two distinct levels in a living room without a trace of discord. Natural rush matting covers the floor's entire upper level, framing the slightly lower central area on all sides. One step down, against a sleek coffee-colored floor, a small area rug the color of distilled sunshine centers attention on the main conversation grouping. It also sparks the room's quiet neutrals and whites without overpowering their subtle effectiveness. Interior design: Barbara D'Arcy.

YEE

1

2

4

5

3

6

AREA DEFINITION

1 A small rya-textured rug, that contrasts vividly with the wall-to-wall carpeting under it, helps a bedroom's foot-of-the-bed sitting area take on more of a living room look. The bold flamestitch-patterned rug earmarks the sitting space and also provides protection for a high-traffic section of the pale carpeting. (Note: the small rug is easier to clean than the entire wall-to-wall stretch.) Interior design: Angelo Donghia of Burge-Donghia.

2 A well-proportioned rug, just under a table-desk (in this case, a Parsons table), defines a part-time working area in a sitting room and makes it look very inviting. The rich pattern of the rug, handmade in Portugal from a Danish pillow-cover design, creates an interesting foil for the expanses of the clear color on walls, the unpatterned upholstery fabrics.

3 The brilliant colors, deep pile and overscaled marble motif of an area rug in the corner of a medium-to-large living room creates an intimate mood, a self-contained feeling, for a corner conversation group. The arresting rug demarcates the space as effectively as a vertical room divider without completely closing it off. Interior design: Inman Cook.

4 A soft white cloud of a rug offers an island of comfort for the bed in a bedroom with a floor that is really too beautiful to hide. The rug provides a cool transition between a brilliant flowered fabric and the warm rosewood finish of the parquet floor. Interior design: Stephen Mallory of Mallory-Tillis.

5 An area rug of important scale visibly reserves a good third of the space in a living room for firegazing and conversation. The rug's loop texture and warm coloring make the hearthside retreat especially cozy. Two deep-seated sofas are placed just beyond the fringe. Interior design: Joseph Braswell.

6 A flamboyant Art Nouveau design under the table accentuates a dining room's welcome. The large-sized area rug, laid over wall-to-wall carpeting, imbues the stately 18th-century mahogany furniture with the fresh, lively look of today. A deeply sculptured pile and brilliant colors emphasize the area rug's swirling pattern and add a marvelous splash of contrast to the room's many hard, smooth surfaces.

FUR ELEGANCE

Dark goat's wool, *below,* in a Greek rug that is a riot of shaggy texture, matches the boldness of the stone wall and rugged beams in a living room which glories in contrasts. The soft ribbed velvet on sofas and chairs is texture of quite another kind, elegant and highly sophisticated. Further unconventional teaming: a crudely carved Spanish bench with a collection of antique French furniture. Neutrals of many hues and values are spiked with bits of pure white—in sofa pillows, in an abstract painting's narrow frame.

Near-white sheepskin, *right,* makes the fluffy and luxurious rug that underwrites an elegant white room. The only pattern is stylized leopard spots on a fabric covering the oversized sofa and an upholstered chair. Plaster palm tree torchères light one wall with great panache, yet detract nothing from a handsome painting. Just beneath it: a collection of Thai ornaments on a white Parsons table. Hi-fi speakers are concealed under two tables that are covered to the floor. Shells and crystal enhance the flamboyancy of a chrome étagère.

LYON

FIREPLACES

**HOW TO
PLAY UP THEIR
INVITING WAYS**

Fireplaces are focal points that establish a hospitable hub in a room, a decorative element, and usually a natural center for a furniture grouping. In contemporary houses a fireplace is most often an integral part of its environment; proportions and materials relate to the architecture. Frequently the hearth is raised or cantilevered to form a shelf for seating or for displaying favorite possessions. Free-standing fireplaces are as carefully shaped as sculpture; witness the one below. In traditional rooms a fireplace, framed with trim and a mantel, makes a graceful base for a handsome composition above it, as shown opposite. If a room has no fireplace, you may be able to install quite easily a free-standing type or a decorative stove that will create both an ambiance and a focal point.

SHULMAN

Contemporary drama, *left:* A big central fireplace in a living room radiates cheer in all directions. And the room's plan for good living radiates from the fireplace which is surrounded by a shallow conversation pit that continues through glass doors onto the terrace. Within the pit: two muted green sofas for sitting and a vivid rainbow-colored stretch of cushioned ledge for perching or lounging. On the upper level: areas for enjoying television, music and games. Architect: William Periera.

Traditional charm, *below:* A simple, beautifully proportioned fireplace— all the more lovely for a handsome pair of andirons and a graceful arrangement of old candelabra, fresh flowers and a treasured mirror—makes the wall itself a decorative delight in a living room where a door on one side keeps the hearth from serving as the focal point of a sitting area. The fireplace furthers the mood of warm hospitality in a sunny room softened by serene blues, brightened by white. Adding to the lightness: the crystal chandelier reflected in the mirror hung high as the door.

LEONARD

BACKGROUNDS
FIREPLACES

The tall opening, *left,* of an
unadorned fireplace, emphasizes
the height of a wall that soars two
stories, balances beautifully with the
slice of balcony on one side, and
reveals every high-leaping blaze.
Relatively carefree: the concrete
tile floor. Architect: John Louis Field.

A stone chimney breast, *below,*
far left, in a study, gives dramatic
importance to the simple fireplace that
matches and backs up to another in
the adjoining living room. The texture
of the rough stone complements an
entire wall of laden bookshelves that
also house the television set and hi-fi.

The tapered shape, *below, center,*
of an enameled stove, adds great
verve to a contemporary room. The
obelisk is set high on a concrete bench
in front of a boldly sectioned wall.

The unusual location, *below,* of
a copper fireplace in front of a
window wall, plus the very striking
silhouette, refreshes the eye with many
delightful compositions (including
a view of drifting snowflakes in season).

BAER

STOLLER

APLIN

GRIGSBY

94

GUERRERO

HARLOW

The raised hearth, *above*, of a gently curved fireplace, brings the fire up to a pleasant level for flame-gazing, and provides enough space for decorative dogs that help make the fireplace a visual joy, flames or no.

A jogged platform, *above, right,* newly added to support an old Dutch stove, was made long enough to include a comfortable nook for sitting and toe-warming in a room that originally lacked a fireplace. Interior design: Anthony Hall.

An invented niche, *right,* welcomes a quaint iron stove into the corner of a bedroom. To make the niche, a board frame is fixed across the corner, and the walls within painted black so they seem to recede more than they do.

GRIGSBY

Chapter 3

SPACE

WAYS TO MAKE THE MOST OF IT

Well-planned space works full time for you on two levels, physical and emotional: it functions efficiently and also makes you feel unfettered and at ease. Whether you have a lot or a little space to work with, the basic challenge is to shape it to your specific needs: your way of life, family activities, preferred kind of entertaining. Of course, your architecture creates advantages or limitations. Today's open plans and expanses of glass require a different approach to interpreting space than do more confined enclosures. This chapter shows easily executed space maneuvers in both new and old houses.

No matter what your particular floor plan, your spatial requirements must meet two demands: flexibility in those rooms where you get together with family and friends for meals and all-around enjoyment, and privacy in bedrooms, bathrooms, work and study areas. The kitchen may fall into either category depending on your approach to preparing meals.

You can literally or figuratively stretch, shape and control space to fit your needs and your life style. A number of space-stretching solutions are based on the efficacy of illusion. If a room *looks* open and expansive, the feeling of spaciousness triumphs over the fact of limited square footage. For example, if a glass window wall is allowed to work its magic without interruption, one is scarcely aware that the room stops where the glass begins. Mirrors cannily used can also work miracles by making rooms seem to multiply two or more times in size.

Shaping and controlling space is possible without changing or moving walls, and, again, this is partly a matter of illusion. Widely spaced uprights or furniture may be used to define, enclose or unite areas on a part-time or permanent basis. A long sofa can separate space so subtly that the suggestion of division may be accepted or ignored at will. On the following pages are many imaginative ways to open up small rooms, make corners inviting, control areas so they provide coziness at times or party settings at others.

Concealing and revealing screen, *right,* does two jobs well: hides ugly windows and a dismal view; creates an illusion of space by reflecting the room in tall panels of mirror. For spatial definition, a white square of tables is framed with sofas and chairs in a roomy but most inviting grouping: Interior design: Alberto Pinto.

MASSEY

PARTITIONS AND DIVISIONS

THAT APPORTION YOUR SPACE

GRIGSBY

A partition can do wonders—create a room within a room or divide large areas into sections without slicing the room apart. If you want to preserve a room's unity and only infer division, you can define certain parts very satisfactorily by understatement, with partitions like these: a short width of sheer ceiling-to-floor curtain; a series of slim uprights; a sofa placed across a room rather than along a wall. Such devices help to keep a room's actual spaciousness intact. A movable screen easily separates areas and can be folded up at will. To give a screen decorative value and minimize its function, hang it with pictures or cover it with handsome paper or fabric.

If you wish, however, to carve out a totally private little enclave—a workroom, for example—choose a partition designed to shut off the area when the fold-back doors, screens or whatever are closed.

Four-fold door, *left,* divides a home office from the adjacent living room. The space for the office was originally a closet— 6 feet by 27 inches—in an apartment that was short on rooms but surprisingly long on storage space. With the folding door open, the office does not seem confining, yet it can be easily closed off before a formal party. Interior design: Jerome Manashaw.

A huge, unframed painting, *left, below,* is hung as a room divider, its size and pattern lending excitement to the simply furnished space. A photo-mural or a striking scenic wallpaper could be used in the same way.

A tall screen, *right,* hides the front door of the apartment from the living room (and vice versa), and also acts as a sharp and major color accent in a room that is otherwise muted in tone. Interior design: Harry Schule and John McCarville.

GRIGSBY

Empire daybed, *left,* makes an elegant divider for a kitchen and dining area: it permits a clear view between guests and the host tossing a salad in the kitchen, and makes a delightful place for relaxing from K.P. duties, planning a meal, or having mid-morning coffee and talk with a drop-in guest. Interior design: Bruce MacIntosh.

A row of supporting posts, *right,* subtly divides a dual-level living room into a cozy fireside area and an airy gathering place. To give the halves unity, dark polished slate paves the entire floor, and the same black and white damask lights up furniture in both sections of the large room. Interior design: Janet Martin Langerman.

Latticework, *below,* makes a small part of a painter's studio a gay setting for meals. Paintings hang on the trellis, and patterned tiles splash color over the floor. Interior design: Jack Johanssen.

DE GENNARO

MAYA

LYON

Bamboo-framed screen, *left,* the same soft white as the surrounding walls, masks an open kitchen at one end of a living room. The screen seems an architectural part of the room since bamboo, instead of conventional wood molding, also frames the nearby window niche and bookcase. Making the screen almost a museum wall: diverse paintings and a prized tole angel facing the living room. The same bamboo-patterned fabric that covers the sofas is laminated to vertical louvers screening the window.

Fish net curtain, *right,* a transparent symbol of a wall, defines living and dining areas without for a second stopping the eye. Wall-to-wall curtains and carpeting are fine room-wideners, and using the window as a wall helps stretch the room, too. The unconventional placement of a sofa bed against the window makes possible a full complement of amenities for living, dining, sleeping, study, within a periphery of only 8 by 16 feet. Interior design: Henry Robert Kann.

Wood grille, *far right,* of pale walnut, is an excellent device for reshaping a long, narrow living room. The grille does not fully block your view, so you can still appreciate the length of the room, yet the division is distinct enough to separate space for a game area. Interior design: T. H. Robsjohn-Gibbings.

SCHNALL

GRIGSBY

GRIGSBY

**SPACE
PARTITIONS AND DIVISIONS**

SPACE
PARTITIONS
AND DIVISIONS

Slender columns, *above,* of painted wood with
accents of colored bottle glass, suggest a
division between a dining room and adjoining sun porch,
yet hide none of the fresh view from dinner guests.
Physically as well as visually the dining room is
expanded for entertaining, since cocktails and
canapés are easily served on the sun porch. But each
room keeps its individuality with its own flooring:
for the porch, a pebble mosaic which quickly sheds
water from the plants; for the dining room,
classic parquet. Interior design: David E. Copeland.

Free-standing bookcases, *right,* of walnut,
reshape the space in a long room, creating
smaller areas that are more comfortable for a library
and a sitting-dining room. The columns, in trios,
are spaced a few inches apart—so they look less
massive—and securely screwed to the floor. At the
top, removable walnut blocks are wedged tightly
into place. Interior design: Clell Bryant Associates.

SPACE STRETCHERS

**THAT MAKE
INCHES
SEEM
LIKE YARDS**

A small room has big possibilities. For one thing, it immediately suggests intimacy and warmth. (People who live in big houses tend to use a little sitting room or study much more than a large drawing room, except when they entertain.) Another plus factor: you can give a small room great decorative charm and style without straining your budget. Use light, clear colors, small patterns, airily designed furniture, simple window treatments—and practice restraint. To save table space, install hanging light fixtures. To make a bed or sofa appear less bulky, match its color or cover to the wall behind it. Above all, make the most of the existing space, vertical as well as horizontal, with built-ins. Build narrow shelves or cupboards in corners; fit them under stairs or eaves. Recess a door, window, narrow seat or piece of furniture by surrounding it with shallow storage. But avoid clutter: leave an area of plain wall to rest the eye, and of open floor for moving around.

BEADLE

Open look, *far left,* of a studio workshop's widely spaced shelves, see-through furniture, and caning patterns (real in the daybed, assumed in the lamp shade, woven into curtains), makes a small but very enterprising room seem airy rather than cluttered. The shelves, narrow ones flanking the window and low ones between tall uprights on the wall, provide storage without looking weighty. Spacewise, too: a hanging lamp that doesn't require valuable table space; slim-legged furniture that reveals most of the floor, so it seems more extensive than it is. Interior design: The Lehmans.

Snug effect, *left,* of tall, protective bookcases and many pillows, makes a small section of wall inviting and private as an inglenook for relaxing. And in the incredibly small area there is open storage for records, too, and cupboards for stashing the unsightly. Walls of the niche are painted sunny yellow, setting it apart from the white built-ins, black and white pillow patterns.

GRIGSBY

GRIGSBY

GUERRERO

BEADLE

Bright strategy, *left,* of hanging a bed canopy over a pair of windows under the eaves, makes twin beds fit nicely into a room that has a minimum of unadulterated wall space. One pattern sweeps over valance, window shades, curtains, walls and bedspreads. The scheme of one light color plus white unifies the mélange of furniture and rickrack of beams. Masking the radiator is a nest of tables.

Disguising pattern, *below,* an all-direction paisley, minimizes the problem proportions and angles of an attic guest room and makes the awkward little space seem desirable. The fabric covers almost everything— window louvers, kite-shaped shade and a lamp shade. Snappy yellow on the floor, radiator and window trim comes from the paisley. The rest: neutrals, white. Interior design: Burt Wayne.

Found space, *left,* between two windows, is converted into a niche that is ample enough for a good-sized dressing table. A large, well-lighted, mirrored panel also opens up the hemmed-in room. Shutters are neat stand-ins for curtains. Unlimited in lightness, freshness: blue and white in several materials and finishes—some bold, some subdued—from floor to ceiling. Interior design: Mallory-Tillis.

Soaring height, *right,* of a two-story living room with limited square footage, is put to such wise use that the area becomes an uncrowded haven, even though it is filled to the brim with books and a collector's mélange. The natural window blind, white brick fireplace and pine bookshelves (cleverly built under the stairs), soar, accenting the vertical dimension. At floor level, rugs from Greece and Spain, two comfortable armchairs, paintings garnered from everywhere, are worthy of the little space each consumes. The background: pine walls slowly turning the color of honey.

SPACE STRETCHERS

LEONARD

CLEVER CORNER TACTICS

**THAT TRANSFORM
LITTLE SPACES
INTO
USEFUL PLACES**

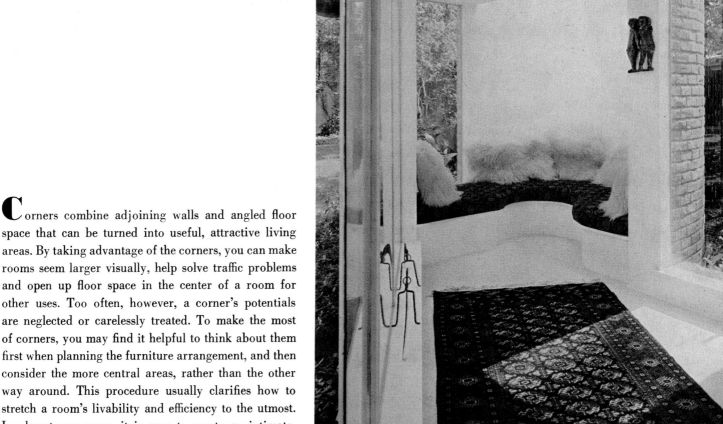

MARIS

orners combine adjoining walls and angled floor space that can be turned into useful, attractive living areas. By taking advantage of the corners, you can make rooms seem larger visually, help solve traffic problems and open up floor space in the center of a room for other uses. Too often, however, a corner's potentials are neglected or carelessly treated. To make the most of corners, you may find it helpful to think about them first when planning the furniture arrangement, and then consider the more central areas, rather than the other way around. This procedure usually clarifies how to stretch a room's livability and efficiency to the utmost. In almost any room, it is easy to create an intimate, little corner retreat for reading or conversation. All you need are two comfortable chairs, a small table and proper lighting. If the space is minuscule, use only one chair and turn the corner into a very personal haven.

In large rooms, banquettes, shelves and cabinets can shape up corners into commodious, special-purpose centers for conversation, work, games or music. Even when a window or jog in a wall makes a corner seem, at first glance, unusable, you can turn the space to good purpose by means of various devices that define the area and provide a backdrop for a furniture grouping. Many simple corner strategies are shown on these four pages.

Inspired angle, *left:* In a tiny living room, a round table makes good capital of a windowed corner. Most of the day the table holds objets d'art and plants, but it easily converts to a work and reading place when cleared of everything except the lamp. At night, the table can be pulled out into the room and set for a cozy dinner for four. The round top is bigger than it looks; the floor-length covering of suede cloth in the same brown as the walls makes the table seem to recede. Light chairs are easy to rearrange for the corner's different purposes. Interior design: Stephen Mallory of Mallory-Tillis.

Rounded corner, *above:* Added onto an almost square room, a snug bay gives a conventional space a far more interesting character. The well-turned corner accommodates a serpentine banquette that seats several for intimate conversation or provides a scenic spot for a daydreaming individual. Rounded addition extends upward into a half-round tower with a slanting skylight. Architects: Clovis Heimsath, Irving Phillips, Jr.

BOUCHER

3

MARGERIN

1

WARD

2

4

MARIS

110

1 Platform bed (a foam rubber mattress on a plywood foundation) was made to fit exactly from corner to corner, making every bit of precious space count in a tiny bedroom. During the day, the bed doubles as a divan, piled with comfort-abetting pillows in both corners. Interior design: Gil Valazquez, Jr.

2 Pull-across bamboo blinds, striped in neutrals, makes a unified backdrop for furniture in a glassed-in corner, turning a difficult-to-use area to good purpose. The coherent background capably sets off sectional sofas in a banquette-like arrangement usually associated with solid walls. The corner's geometrics include the hexagon of the coffee table, the squares of the rug and pillow and the rounds of the backrests. Interior design: Richard Himmel.

3 Spiral staircase, a magnificent example of 19th-century ironwork, was unearthed in a farmyard, and literally corkscrewed into one corner of a small, remodeled carriage house. The space-saving stairs link the living room with the studio above, give style to what could have been a plain-Jane area. Shallow bookcase and a round table add to the corner's new-found usefulness.

4 An architect's forethought fits a stone fireplace neatly into one corner of the master bedroom in a seaside house. The elevated hearth is in full view even from the bed. The room also enjoys a wide green vista through its sliding glass doors, but drawing the curtains and lighting a warming fire in the corner transforms the room into a snug retreat. Equal in boldness to the stonework is the massive French-Canadian armoire on the adjacent wall, where it has all the door-swinging space it needs. Architect: Harry Bates.

5 A richly detailed, mural wallpaper defines a library corner in a small living room. The scene's marvelous perspective seems to open up the space, making the room appear larger. A shelf skirts the corner at dado height, holds decorative treasures that convey the same period feeling as the wall design. Interior design: Barbara D'Arcy.

6 Curtains drawn all the way around a windowed corner make a background for a sitting room arrangement in a master bedroom. When the flower-sprigged overcurtains are drawn back, the continuous valance gives unity to the corner. The small area contains a good deal of furniture yet manages to look airy, because all the non-upholstered pieces are trim, colors are light, pattern is lively but not too dominant. Interior design: Norman McD. Foster.

5
GRIGSBY

6
LEONARD

MIRRORS

Mirrors are multipliers of space and of any object they reflect. One mirrored wall visually doubles a room's length or width. Two mirrored walls stretch the room in all directions. If you place a piece of furniture or an ornament close to a mirror, you can see it and its reflection at the same time—with expansive results. For example, a chandelier becomes a pair; a small table butted up against mirror looks like a banquet table; two facing chairs turn into a group.

To emphasize the illusion of walking "through the looking glass," use large sheets of mirror that extend from ceiling to floor and that cover an entire wall. The fewer seams, the more convincing the effect. To open up a leafy vista on a solid wall, hang a big mirror opposite a window that has a pretty view. To create a "mirror picture," hang a framed mirror on a mirrored wall; the frame defines a composition! To distract the eye from a necessary partition, mirror it. And to offset the cool glitter of silvery glass, introduce a wealth of warm colors and lush textures.

LEONARD

MARIS

Great reflection, *above,* in a wall mirrored—not from the baseboard but from the floor itself—to the ceiling, visually doubles the size of a small sitting room. It also plays to the hilt the exuberant patterns of the flocked silk wall covering and the Tabriz rug. Interior design: Everett Brown.

Space extenders, *left,* a slim pair of black-framed Victorian mirrors, are hung on adjacent walls of a tiny powder room, where they also serve as lengthy looking glasses. Another plus: their lively shimmer adds snap to the space-stretching scheme of black and white.

Scenic sparkle, *right,* of three zigzag walls sheathed with mirror, makes an L-shaped dining loggia seem absolutely limitless, marvelously bright, endlessly beautiful. The huge panels reflect every bit of the whiteness and the intricate patterns of orchid plants inside, plus the deep greens of gardens visible through glass doors and windows on the loggia's other walls. Sharpening the perspective: framed mirrors hung on two of the mirrored walls. To keep the illusion of space under control: floor borders of black; baseboards of contrasting white.

GRIGSBY

GRIGSBY

BEADLE

MASSEY

Added depth, *above,* plus endless beauty, are provided by a fireplace wall paneled with mirror and then embellished with a Venetian mirror-framed mirror. Stepping up the bright look is one clear color lightened with white. Threefold screens hide ugly corner jogs and also stand in for overcurtains.

A new view, *above, right,* brightens the dining room of a city apartment, thanks to mirrored window shutters that flank a mirrored wall panel. The shutters hide anti-prowler gates without blocking access to a fire escape, and repeat—in the bargain—the walls' flame-stitch design, heightening its effect by adding new angles to the pattern. Interior design: Bebe Winkler.

Corner deception, *right,* is practiced by a screen with four mirrored panels. The mirrors cleverly play back part of the scene, so the corner seems to play an active part in the room. The screen also helps lure the eye from the broken lines of a windows-and-radiator wall. Another wile: airy curtains over Roman shades provide a sense of depth, making the room seem larger. Interior design: Ripley Rogers.

GRIGSBY

Grand illusions, *above,* of spaciousness are conjured up in a very small living room by mirrored panels completely lining two of its sides. The bright glitter also gives a mercurial lift to the neutral scheme of pale blonds and off-whites. In turn, the neutrals' many rich textures add interest to all the glossiness—of the mirror, black lacquered chairs, glass-topped coffee table. Two sofas are arranged banquette fashion to make the most of the room's real dimensions. Interior design: Louis Fischer.

Narcissistic image, *right,* in a mirrored end wall, helps the pencil-slim L of an apartment living room masquerade as a full-blown dining room. Upon reflection, the table hardly seems to be tight against the wall, and the simple wall sconces become round as chandeliers. Shutters lend far-reaching outdoor connotations to balcony doors. Keeping furnishings to a minimum (no rug, no curtains) is another space-stretcher. Interior design: Leif B. Pedersen.

SEATING STRATEGY

Furniture arrangement defines space and influences social behavior. This is especially true in living rooms and areas where seating groups play the major role. You can use them to unite or divide space, direct traffic and establish where and how people can gather in comfort. Seating should be both flexible and congenial; even an isolated chair for reading should not be too remote. Because today's floor plans tend to be very open, traditional approaches to furniture arrangement no longer necessarily work. Big reaches of glass or space require that seating groups stand on their own rather than rely on solid walls for background. Sofas, chairs and accompanying tables often form islands for relaxation, subtly connected so they can be enlarged, reduced or merged on occasion. Contemporary upholstered pieces are so low that they barely interrupt the sweep of space around them; see-through tables have the same effect; so do conversation pits. Sofas are designed to look well from every angle because they are so often visible on all sides, with nothing to mask backs and ends.

In any room, old or new, seating should have an inviting, sociable quality. Whether it is anchored to a wall or not, a grouping should be open and accessible but subtly encircling. It should welcome one or two or a chatty group. Light pull-up chairs, stools or big floor cushions are essential for flexibility, because they can be easily moved from one place to another. Tables should be conveniently placed to hold glasses, ashtrays, whatever; a table behind a free-standing sofa can relate two areas. The seating arrangements on these pages all deftly shape space and draw people together.

GRIGSBY

A wall-free group, *right,* of upholstered pieces and accompanying tables, forms an inviting place for conversation without one solid wall for a backdrop. The great expanses of glass, with their marvelous views, dictate an away-from-the-walls arrangement and also govern the height of the furniture— low so it emphasizes the sweep of space. Comfortable furniture makes its point in front of the fireplace, which is flanked by bay windows. Chairs and sofas with straight backs, and simply shaped tables take easily to a right-angle arrangement, pleasing to look at from all sides. Important for holding together this type of seating plan: an eye-catching area rug (the fur is the most richly textured of the room's many neutrals). Note how the out-in-the-open group is unencumbered by lamp cords; all light comes from ceiling fixtures, plotted to focus on furniture and sculpture. At the opposite end of the room, *left,* quite another space-defining story: wall-hugging banquettes take full advantage of an alcove's three walls. This very unified group gives the room its only swack of vivid color—a definite lure for a place apart.

GRIGSBY

A commodious ledge, *below,* is built into a living room at the end originally intended for dining, subtly separating the area for luxurious lounging. The wall-to-wall nook, partly cushioned, makes an inviting private spot to curl up with a book away from the living room proper, but during parties the open alcove (with plants pushed aside) provides extra seating space for guests. At night a chandelier, hung low over a side table, brings a cozy glow to the snuggery. Interior design: Ward Bennett.

Low geometric shapes, *right,* combined into floor-hugging furniture, keep the focus down, giving the intimate feeling of a step-down conversation pit. Yet the low-ceilinged room actually has no differences in its floor level. Bright colors and forms—gay as kindergarten play equipment—are allied to make normal-height seats comfortable for conversation and convenient to games and a record player. Cubes between chairs can be sat on or, topped with marble, used as tables. For more gaiety: carpeting that also plays games with lively shapes and colors.

Two levels, *bottom right,* of
furniture, distinctly divide a living
room's space into a U-shaped
concentration of low seating, and
a high wall array of books, bibelots and
music equipment. Color and texture
play up the separation: the
brights are confined to the conversation
pit where the inviting look of hot
pinks is further boosted by the
warmth of velvet. Cooling the
exuberance of the pinks: white walls,
open shelving and polished
slate flooring on the upper level.

LYON

LYON

Three cool couches, *above,* icy blue, and backless to let breezes go by, set apart a windowed alcove for warm weather relaxing. Easily moved pull-up chairs provide extra seating for a party. Instead of curtains, sliding wood grilles made in Morocco create a filigree of light and a Mediterranean mood. Interior design: Michael Taylor.

A lengthy divan, *left,* takes a slim bit of space along a window wall and, with the aid of simple wicker chairs, forms a separate gathering place in a living room. Window shutters and a space divider are finely made, latticed wood panels lined with thin silk to cast a rosy glow. Cushions are covered in scraps from worn antique rugs. The ambiance is North African and romantic. Interior design: Robert K. McNie.

A curve of sofas, *right, top,* under an airy vault of stretch nylon, lures guests to one gregarious circle. The off-white of the sofas forms a calm core for lively parties and also helps the large pieces to merge with the near-white surroundings. Other pleasant curves worth noting: those of the hovering lamp, the lazy Susan table and the rosewood and steel tables that ring the seating group. Interior design: Milo Baughman.

Linked platforms, *far right, top,* and upholstered banquettes form a U around a terra-cotta lacquer table to furnish a cozy Persian-inspired alcove. The warm colors and friendly arrangement create an intimate atmosphere, a protected feeling. Rich patterns and three Oriental rugs lend the requisite air of splendor. Interior design: Milo Baughman.

Adaptable hassocks, *right,* between sofas and the fireplace, keep the view clear and give guests a choice of facing a sofa-based or hearthside conversation group. Small coffee tables contribute to the room's open look and also simplify traffic. By the fireplace, a tall screen lends importance to a little furniture group and balances a bookcase in a corner planned for reading or tête-à-têtes. Interior design: Falasco-Smith.

MASSEY

MASSEY

GRIGSBY

Free-standing components, *right,*
are assembled to form a genial
approximation of a conversation pit
without a single structural change
in the room. Arrayed around a strongly
patterned area rug in an otherwise neutral
room, a related series of platforms,
cushions, chair backs, pillows and trays
are visually held together by the rug's
brilliant coloring and stark shapes. A bold
collage, dramatic focus for the furniture
formation, rests on an antique French easel.

Matching trio, *below,* of two chairs
and an ottoman, forms a toe-to-toe
stretch across the library end of a sizable
living room. Cutting a color swathe
across the mostly white room, the
unusual arrangement sets aside the fireplace
area for reading in comfort. Books
on shelves, so readily accessible, are
apt to be in demand any hour
of the day. Interior design: Edmund Motyka.

SILVA

FOTIADES

Chapter 4

LIGHTING NATURAL AND ARTIFICIAL

As much as color, shape and texture, light is an element of decoration. When lighting is poor, no effort to create beauty, comfort and practicality can succeed. Yet, until recent times, the role of lighting in interior design was largely ignored. The revolutionary last few years have changed all that. In a flight of imagination and technology, we have arrived at the certainty that light is important in every aspect of our visual lives. Paying audiences attend light shows; crowded galleries display the works of luminary artists. Exciting and functional, natural and artificial light in the home is now a major consideration in an architect's plans, and there is even a flourishing profession: lighting consultant. Builders and re-modelers draw on a varied stock of ready-made skylights that is increasing, and the distinguished designers who concentrate their talents on lamps and fixtures now find themselves starring in museum displays.

In any room, two kinds of light are required: general diffuse light to illuminate the space, and concentrated light where needed for activities or displaying objects. Daylight is ideal general lighting; except for the tropics or the western exposure on summer afternoons, you can't have too much of it. When daylight seems excessive, shutters, shades or curtains can control it easily. General artificial lighting tries to approach a daylight effect by providing soft and uniform light without harsh shadows and often without a visible light source. Techniques include luminous ceilings, cove or cornice lighting, partly hooded ceiling fixtures that wash a wall with light, and large area modular elements such as recessed ceiling down-lights around the perimeter of a room. Experts recommend that general lighting be controlled by dimmers, so that mood can be adjusted from a high level which is brilliant and stimulating, to a low level which is intimate and soothing. General lighting alone is monotonous and limited. For the charm of variety created by gentle shadows and pools of light and for practical direct beams on a book or a desk or a kitchen counter, we add lamps and fixtures. For a new esthetic adventure, we can also decorate with light.

BEADLE

A huge skylight, *left,* thrusting upward to follow the roofline, bathes a living room with day-long light that changes with the hour and provides a slow-motion tonal show on the white surfaces which line the room. Moonlight and star patterns are the evening fare, until the overhead spotlights are switched on. Behind the free-standing fireplace wall is a dining room flooded with window light which adds to the lambency of the living room.

Two kinds of ceiling light, *right,* make a foyer glow. Under a vast, framed rectangle of cove lighting, a four-sided parade of recessed spotlights forms a border. Gleaming below are walls sheathed in silver leaf which performs multiple feats of reflection behind paintings and sculptures. Interior design: Edward Benesch.

LAUTMAN

OVERHEAD LIGHT SOURCES

The old-fashioned overhead fixture, the chandelier, was well designed for candles, gas jets or oil. But when enough electric bulbs are installed in such a fixture to shed adequate light, the glare is unattractive and a strain on the eye. Modern designers reserve chandeliers as low-wattage elements of decoration and provide overhead lighting of a very different sort, well illustrated on these next six pages. The forms vary, but whether the light is natural or artificial it is diffuse and designed to bathe all corners of the room with a glarefree, even glow. The venerable skylight—a breathtaking feature in the world's oldest intact building, the Pantheon—is enjoying a great revival today as an overhead source of natural light. You can get ready-made skylights in a variety of materials (plastic, glass, some with screens and opening devices), shapes and sizes, and you can install artificial lights inside them for night use. A luminous ceiling resembles a skylight, but its light is man-made. Overhead light reduces the number of lamps needed in a room, so you can use concentrated light only if necessary or pleasing.

NAAR

BEADLE

LYON

YEE

Luminous ceiling, *far left,* the one source of light in a large, well-organized kitchen, floods the central work island and every part of the room evenly. The neat grid overhead also fits in with the cane-patterned wallpaper and brick-like vinyl floor tiles. Architect: Donald E. Nick. Interior design: Rosemary Robinson.

A pyramid of glass, *left,* cut into the roof of an old city house, opens a windowless kitchen to the sun. For concentrated work area light, a trio of shaded hanging fixtures bright against a turkey red wall. Shallow shelf above the counter utilizes often-wasted space.

A classic studio skylight, *above left,* over a top floor dining room, makes it possible to grow an indoor garden. Not only sunlight but moonlight beams down here, and air can be let in with the flick of a switch. Austrian shade cuts glare. Architect: Roy Starbird.

Bountiful window, *above right,* replaces much of the pitched roof in a remodeled house. The stargazer's skylight, installed in the bed alcove, has a pull-up shade to temper daytime glare. Architect: Geysa Sarkany.

Panel of light, *right,* illuminates a foyer that doubles as a miniature museum. The marble section sunk into the teak floor reflects and steps up the intensity of the luminous ceiling. Architect: Arthur L. Finn.

GRIGSBY

Circles of light, *left,* in the ceiling of a
bathroom, provide two kinds of illumination.
Three large circles are skylights for the daytime;
the smaller circles are artificial lights
both for general illumination at night
and for a close look at the grooming process
at any time. Mosaic tiles on the built-in
dressing table and lavatory counters
make an interesting counterpoint to the
sleek redwood paneling and cabinets,
the pale carpeting. Architect: Edward D. Dart.

Glowing rafters, *right,* are a totally new
idea for flooding a room with brightness.
Fluorescent tubes are boxed into beams that
start high and reach still higher so that their
pattern doesn't distract the cook below. Yet
the streaks of light, controlled by dimmers, are
fascinating to look at, as are the fan-shaped
shadows behind. Architects: Charles
Moore/William Turnbull and Rurik Ekstrom.

LIGHTING
OVERHEAD SOURCES

Multiple movable units on a track, *below,* used here for the kitchen area
of a family room, provide a flexible form of general lighting that was
first popular in store displays. Commercial lighting, which has to be effective
if business is to flourish, has sparked the ideas of many modern lighting designers.
To the contemporary eye, the undisguised practicality of exposed track
lighting is not only totally acceptable, but also considered decorative and suitable.

Clerestory plus ceiling bulbs, *right,* shed light from above in this all-purpose
party and guest room. In addition, more natural light flows through tall
windows at the left, and more artificial light comes from wall fixtures in the
sofa-bed niche. Fascinating ceiling lighting consists of twelve light tracks on
which frosted 25-watt bulbs can be moved into endless new patterns between cedar slats.

BAER

GRIGSBY

LAMPS AND FIXTURES

CONCENTRATED LIGHT

No matter how good general lighting is, it must be supplemented by the concentrated light that lamps and fixtures provide. A well-accessorized room might do without the presence of unlighted lamps, but it cannot do without the excitement and changes that areas of light and shadow bring. Concentrated light may hang from the ceiling, reach out from the wall, stand on the floor or on a piece of furniture. Stylistically, its varieties are as limitless as the periods of design and the inventiveness of individual designers. You choose your lamps as you do any accessory: to harmonize or contrast with the general feeling of the room. But when you are lighting for what the lighting consultant calls "serious visual tasks"— reading, sewing—be sure there is adequate directed light that allows a person to sit in comfort without his head or body casting any shadows on his work.

MASSEY

HILL

A cluster of bulbs, *above*, frankly showing their hardware store sockets and plugs, is assembled in a chandelier that hangs above the table in a red dining room.

Big white globes, *right*, on stem-slim stands and girdled with thin metal, give concentrated light to a dining area at night. A candle in a hurricane globe on the table, and others in a white torchère against the wall, add a flickering gaiety to evenings in the entirely white-lined room.

Arc-borne light, *opposite*, travels such a sweep that it acts as a spotlight beaming down from above. Also used over today's dining tables, here it brightens a bedroom-sitting room, and is silhouetted boldly against bare walls. In total harmony with molded plastic, contemporary furniture, it complements the vibrant green print.

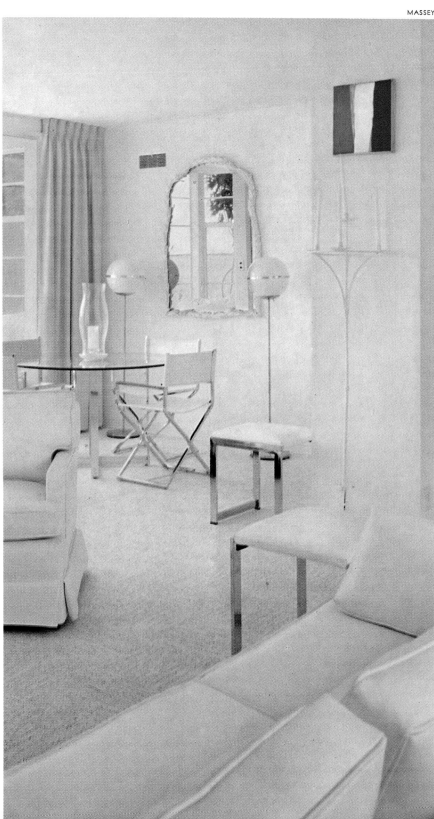

GRIGSBY

2

BEADLE

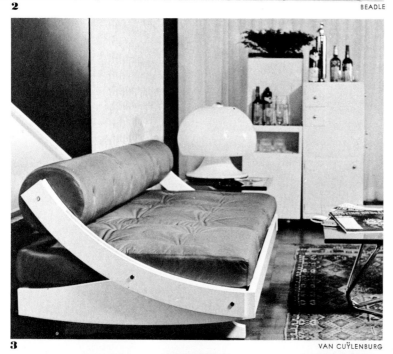

3

VAN CUŸLENBURG

1

BEADLE

LIGHTING
LAMPS AND FIXTURES

1 Two white plaster lamps, designed by the distinguished Swiss sculptor Giacometti, are wonderful, clean shapes in a room containing elaborately detailed screens, furniture and accessories. These lamps complement most decorative periods.

2 A lamp originally designed for architectural drafting adjusts in every direction and casts an excellent light for a variety of tasks. Made in sleek chrome, it has great style and is finding a place in many homes. The base can be a stand or a clamp.

3 The mushroom is a favorite lamp shape and most often, like this one, has a translucent shade that glows evenly without bright spots where the bulbs are. Resultant light is soft, diffuse.

4 This little lamp provides a charming spot of orangey gleam wherever it stands and may be combined with one or two more for a bit of luminal art. The material is a translucent plastic.

5 There is a very new look to this simple, fat ceramic lamp whose shape is the ultimate in roundness. The shade, made of paper, is another aspect of roundness: the cylinder. Both whites are matte.

6 Adjustable cylinder lamps are useful because they can direct a beam right on a book or a piece of needlework, while additional light is cast upward for general room illumination. Here in a bedroom for two, each bed has a movable pole-mounted light.

7 Three kinds of traditional lighting further the mellow mood of a room furnished with antiques: a chandelier with candle-like bulbs, a sconce with real candles, and a candlestick table lamp.

8 Wall-mounted swing-arm lamps, small and finely made, with metal tubing enclosing the wire, are often used in pairs, flanking a sofa as in this living room, or on either side of a fireplace or double bed. The fixtures are made of chrome or brass.

9 Bases of clear glass are an old tradition enjoying a big revival. Glass has the valuable quality of not interrupting the color or pattern behind it while bringing a sparkle of its own.

4   VAN CUŸLENBURG   5   VAN CUŸLENBURG

6

8

7

9

DECORATING WITH LIGHT

Not only has contemporary design brought us new ways to enjoy comfortable and attractive, general and concentrated lighting in our rooms, but it has also brought us a wonderful playful attitude toward light for its own sake, light as a decoration. The new radiant revolution gives us light built into floors, lamps that are pure luminescence from top to bottom, tables that seem to contain a miniature sun, tubes and shapes filled with light that stand in for painting and sculpture. Now fitted with dimmers, big bare bulbs that once were painstakingly concealed, today stand proudly in plain sight. From the diffuse glow of some of the decorative lights to the twinkling pinpoints of others come an aliveness and gaiety that we have always loved in open fireplaces, in soft gaslit globes and in the tongues of candle flame. Finally we have beautified electricity.

A gallery of lights, *right,* is a short, apt description of this apartment living room. Three glass-topped tables wrapped in black vinyl send soft light upward. Cantilevered, round glass cocktail tables are ringed with little bulbs underneath. In the background on the foyer wall, a glass-topped white box illuminates a painting above it. Concealed sources beam light on other pictures, while twin black columns direct shafts of light upward. Enhancing the light play are vinyl surfaces and velvet walls. Interior design: Robert B. Becker.

MASSEY

A glowing globe, *top,* is one geometric in this fascinating, handily small chairside table. Around it is a cylinder of Plexiglas, and the top is a third shape: a round slice of glass.

A light floor, *above,* is probably the most radical innovation in the radiant revolution. Here, under glass, is a glimmering combination of neon and fluorescent tubes. Mirrored walls intensify effect. Interior design: Lila Katzen.

LIGHTING
DECORATING WITH LIGHT

GRIGSBY

Luminal sculpture, *left,* made of neon tubes, hangs from a stairwell ceiling so that its exciting colors, unusual form and the shadows it casts can be seen from many vantage points.

Fire-like changes, *right, top,* fascinate the eye and intrigue the imagination as flashing colored light is produced by programmed shapes around fixed bulbs.

Decorative lights, *below,* in a Roman apartment, dominate where the furniture is simple and white, the walls devoid of other ornaments. The luminal decorations consist of a light sculpture on the wall and a scattering of glowing cubes. The sitting area is tucked under a balcony in a vast palazzo drawing room, marked by an Indian rug and a wall of plants.

PRIMOIS

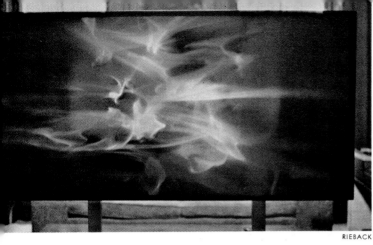

Gem-cut prism, *below,* made
of acrylic, refracts and
intensifies the light beamed
up from below and is
interesting to view from all angles.

Gigantic jewel, *above,* simply
carved acrylic form enclosed
within two acrylic boxes,
is lit by an up-shining white light.

Light painting, *below,* over a
mantel, glows in programmed
pattern. Its official name
is "Sequencia Visual
P-53"; its effect is dreamlike.

Neon figure, *above,* flashing off
and on rhythmically, introduces
a contemporary focal point of color,
line and light to the classic
setting of an artist's lovely garden.

139

LIGHTING
DECORATING WITH LIGHT:
SWITCHED-ON COLOR CHANGES

In addition to lighting's steady job of bringing general and concentrated illumination to a room, and of influencing mood with the placement and variety of light sources, an exciting new role has been added. Borrowing from stagecraft, home lighting can now project color and pattern and movement into the atmosphere. With a twirl of a control button, rooms can be washed or dappled with any hue or intensity of color, evoking different seasons of the year and times of day, and ranging from hypnotically soothing to amusingly bizarre, with a wide gamut in between. Like music, light painting is mood-reflecting and mood-producing. Like music, it can be changed easily and, when you have had enough, turned off. You can now enjoy the pleasure of evoking whatever ambiance you wish and, as you have seen dozens of times on stage at the theater, the way a set is lit creates the emotional climate.

Simulated moonlight, *left,* is achieved with two tubes of black light (whose rays make many materials glow) hidden at the base of the twin niches that flank the fireplace. Here, glowing turquoise, the left niche is seen. The light hits each phosphorescent-painted panel and also plays on the nylon jersey shell stretched over giant hoops skimming the ceiling. Interior design: Jack Lenor Larsen.

Black light, *right,* changes all in a party setting where everything else is unchanged. Under normal lighting, seen at the top, colors are natural and familiar and pleasant enough, but under black light, seen below, a wonderfully dreamlike air of make-believe takes over. Tubes for black light, whose even glow is bluish, are tucked beneath the floor's edge.

GRIGSBY

GRIGSBY

GRIGSBY

Chapter 5

400 YEARS OF FURNITURE DESIGN

Mixing the furniture of the present and the past with a free hand has become so much the rule that it is rare today to see a preponderance of antiques in a room without some contrasting note of the contemporary, or a preponderance of modern furniture without some traditional accent. To our late 20th-century eyes, antiques seem to need a contemporary fillip to give them vitality, and contemporary rooms to call for a touch of the past to give them stability and warmth. It is not at all extraordinary, in fact, to find in one room a mixture that spans four centuries of design, for we have learned that neither the date nor the country of origin is any criterion of what goes with what.

Far more important in composing a compatible mixture is whether each design is good of its kind; whether it is appropriate in scale for the spot where you mean to place it (a lofty highboy might add stature to a small room, yet look awkward and cramped if pushed into the corner of a large one); and how well it serves its purpose.

One other consideration that can be a helpful guide in mixing old and new is the relative degree of elegance. In every period before 1900, there existed two types of design that developed more or less independently. In 18th-century France, for instance, there was a marked difference between the elaborate furniture turned out for the court by the cabinetmakers of Paris and the simpler, sturdier "provincial" that furnished the châteaus and farmhouses of the countryside. During the same period, the fashionable cabinetmakers of London and Colonial Philadelphia and Newport were executing designs that had little in common with the English country furniture or the simple pine and maple pieces we usually mean when we say "Early American." Even in 19th-century America, there was a distinct difference between the elegant and sometimes over-elaborate work of Duncan Phyfe, Lannuier and Belter and the modest spool-turned furniture later labeled "cottage." As a general rule, the provincial designs of all countries and all periods have a definite affinity and tend to mix with each other more smoothly than they do with any of the once fashionable styles.

On the next twelve pages is a design review of the 17th, 18th and 19th centuries and most of the 20th. While necessarily incomplete (whole books have been written about each period), the roster is a representative sampling of the furniture designs most characteristic of their own day, most influential on future periods and those most widely reproduced or adapted today.

The old and the new, *right,* mix happily in the living room of a New York brownstone. Although the background details —crystal chandelier, ceiling molding, lambrequins above the window—are traditional, much of the furniture is modern. The upholstered chair and sofa are the slimmed-down variety that came in after World War II. The directors' chairs, fancied up with a painted bamboo finish, are the type that was elevated from yacht deck to living room in the 1950s, and the steel and glass coffee table speaks clearly of the 1960s. Yet they combine easily and comfortably with the cane-back sofa, rush-seat chairs and game table—all Italian antiques. Interior design: Audrey Kohler.

17th CENTURY

The 17th century was a century of beginnings. New lands were being explored and settled, and new wealth was pouring into Europe. Until well into the 1600s, furniture design was dominated by the elegance of the Renaissance. But that gradually evolved into the full-blown baroque, a style that originated in Italian architecture. From Italy, baroque moved on to France, Holland, England and America, changing character as it went and taking on new forms.

The fashionable styles of this period were also reflected in simple pieces created for people who, a century earlier, would have been satisfied with a crude stool, a box-like chest and straw bedding. Just as carving, veneering and gilding characterized the court furniture, these simpler pieces were distinguished by boldness of line, turning and painted decorations and finishes.

Another innovation of the 17th century was that, for the first time, people began to expect comfort in furniture. They also began to think about its artistic aspects as well as its strictly practical functions. By the end of the century most of the furniture forms we know today had made their appearance (as you will see on these four pages) and were ready for the refinements they received from the brilliantly talented cabinetmakers of the great decorative age that followed.

Although 17th-century styles were pretty well out of fashion from the mid-nineteen twenties until the mid-sixties, they have recently been revived, especially for rooms with a Mediterranean flavor. Designs such as the farthingale chair, opposite page, and the paneled chests and cupboards on page 147 have been widely reproduced or adapted. Among antiques, even the crudest American designs of this period, often called "the Pilgrim century," usually bring prices too steep for anyone but the most affluent collectors.

Beds

During the 17th century, beds, which previously had been built into alcoves, began to resemble our free-standing beds.

1

Low-post bed with carved headboard appeared in southern countries like Spain.

2

Built-in paneled beds, with storage in foot and curtains to keep out drafts, were still the rule in colder countries.

3

The two-part trundle bed, with low posts and headboard but high legs, became popular in America as a space-saver.

Stools

Throughout the 17th century, the stool was perhaps the most widely used of all furniture, since the few chairs in each house were reserved for the master and honored guests.

1

The simple "joined" or "coffin" stool, with turned legs, board top and sturdy stretchers, was common in England and America.

2

The later, more aristocratic French upholstered stool had elaborately carved legs and feet.

3

Charles II stool combined cushioned top with turned legs and stretchers—an English version of Flemish baroque.

RIEGER

Early Chairs

During the first years of the century, chairs were made for the most part in traditional designs dating back to the Middle Ages. Scant attention was paid to comfort, apart from a back to lean against.

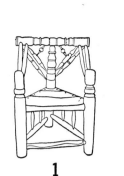

1

The turned chair with triangular seat was little more than a three-legged stool with a back added.

2

Later turned chair, with front legs that continued up to support arms, was better looking, a bit more comfortable.

3

Early American ladder-backs were simpler because first settlers had no time for frills such as turning.

Later Chairs

After 1850, chairs became more comfortable, more elegant and—following the restoration of Charles II—more elaborate. Cane seats and backs came in about 1665.

1

The panel-back or wainscot chair had developed originally from the built-in chair stall. The back was sometimes carved in linen-fold pattern.

2

English country chair was modified panel-back, lighter in weight with thinner seat and more elaborately turned legs.

3

French Burgundian chair had boldly shaped slats instead of a solid back, and seat was upholstered in needlepoint.

4

The farthingale or Cromwellian chair was designed specifically to accommodate exaggerated hoopskirts.

Armless, it had a high, wide upholstered seat, a low upholstered back, turned legs and stretchers.

5

Spanish chairs had geometrically carved stretchers, small paw-like feet, velvet seats and backs finished with nailheads.

6

Portugal's contribution was a flared, fluted foot, first adopted by Flemish baroque, later by the English and Americans.

7

Charles II, back from exile in Holland, introduced into England the ornately carved and caned armchair named after him.

8

American version of Charles II chair was, like all American adaptations of London styles, less ornate and in many ways more graceful.

Settees and Daybeds

The earliest type of seating for two or more was a stool extended into a bench. High-backed wainscoted benches or settees were used in the great halls.

1

American Colonial bench, with lower back, shaped arms, turned spindles and simple straight legs, came along later.

2

Charles II settee was simply two Charles II chairs joined to form a double seat.

3

Earliest type of chaise longue or daybed was an extended chair with cane back and seat.

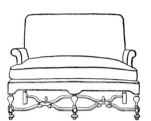

4

William and Mary bench-settee offered more comfort: upholstered seat, back and arms, usually covered with crewelwork.

5

French upholstered bench was enlarged to nearly the size and shape of today's sofa.

Tables

During the 17th century, tables became more varied—large ones for dining, smaller ones for serving, writing, cards. In England, oak gradually gave way to walnut.

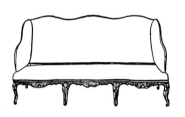

1

Jacobean stretcher table with carved apron and plain stretchers was usually made of oak.

2

Spanish oak tables with elaborately carved drawers and turned legs often had iron stretchers.

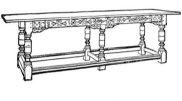

3

English oval tables with curved stretchers—sometimes of walnut—began to appear about mid-century.

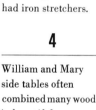

4

William and Mary side tables often combined many woods in beautiful marquetry patterns. Country-made versions were decorated with paint.

5

American butterfly table had wing-like supports to hold up the drop leaves.

6

Gate-leg tables, so called because of gate-like supports for leaves, became popular during second half of century when rooms were first set aside for dining.

Chests and Highboys

Original storage furniture consisted of simple chests or boxes raised from the floor on straight legs. Later, drawers were added at bottom, and finally box disappeared.

1

English Jacobean chests were usually of oak with geometrically carved panels.

2

Italian chests were far more decorative, often so carved and paneled that little flat surface remained.

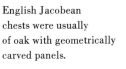

3

"Connecticut chest" of transitional box-plus-drawers type was ornamented with split spindles, painted black.

4

First highboys dispensed with box, had an extra drawer below main section and taller legs. Shaped front stretcher, turned legs and ball feet of this American design are typical of William and Mary style.

Commodes and Lowboys

The chest of drawers or commode rested on feet without legs. The lowboy—half chest, half table—often served as a base for a higher chest.

1

New England country chests on ball feet were decorated with carved molding and paneling plus painted motifs.

2

Louis XIV commode, with metal mounts on drawers and frame and hoof feet, typified elegance of French court furniture.

3

William and Mary lowboy had continuous stretcher, connecting as many as six or eight legs.

4

American lowboy or dressing table of same period was simpler, having only one drawer and four legs with crossed stretchers.

Cupboards

Cupboards were basically chests that opened at the front rather than the top.

1

Hall and parlor cupboard, sometimes called a press cupboard, stored cups, goblets and silver rather than clothes.

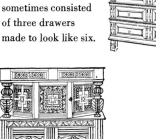

2

In American press cupboard, lower part sometimes consisted of three drawers made to look like six.

3

Credenzas, longer and lower than cupboards and elaborately paneled, originated in Italy.

4

A *credenzina* or little credenza with one door and one drawer often looked like one section of a larger piece.

Writing Desks

A new form of furniture that emerged during the century was the desk. From the writing box on stand, it evolved to a form very close to the secretary.

1

Desk-on-frame in William and Mary style was designed for stand-up writing.

2-3

Cabinet desk with drawer below writing section came next. English version, *far left*, was decorated with marquetry, while American version, *left*, was embellished with painted motifs.

4

Kneehole desk with center recess was an elegant addition to French court furniture. Some were lavishly decorated with metal inlay technique invented by the royal designer, André Charles Boulle.

5

New York fall-front desk, a close forerunner of the secretary, combined writing cabinet with chest of drawers.

6

English fall-front desk of William and Mary period was often decorated with floral marquetry.

147

18ᵗʰ CENTURY

The 18th century was a decorative arts century, one of the richest the world has known. People were ready for the comforts of furniture and houses designed to reflect the elaborate social customs of the day. The fashion pendulum swung from the early flamboyant baroque to the exuberant rococo of the mid-1700s and on to the simplicity and discipline of neoclassicism.

Designers and craftsmen came into their own, and four great names, all from England, are widely honored to this day: Thomas Chippendale; the brothers Adam; George Hepplewhite; and Thomas Sheraton. But styles were also named for the monarchs of the period —Anne and the Georges in England and the Regent Louis XV, and Louis XVI in France. For the most part, these styles overlapped or merged gradually into one another. But in the last quarter of the century, the delicate neoclassicism of the English architect-designer Robert Adam, inspired by the discoveries of the ruins at Herculaneum and Pompeii, brought into fashion a new vocabulary of design.

The American colonies adopted the styles of the mother country, adapting and refining them, usually simplifying them. In the flourishing seaboard cities were many skilled and talented cabinetmakers such as William Savery in Philadelphia and the Townsend-Goddard family in Newport.

Since they were first created, 18th-century furniture designs have almost never been wholly forgotten. In America, small city and country cabinetmakers continued to adapt Chippendale, Hepplewhite and Sheraton long after their more fashionable contemporaries in New York and Baltimore had gone on to something new. And many reproductions of 18th-century designs were made for the Philadelphia Centennial Exposition of 1876. Today, some of these "Centennial pieces" are hard for an amateur to distinguish from furniture made a century earlier. Currently, French furniture of the 18th century brings the highest prices, closely followed by high quality American 18th-century antiques.

RIEGER

French Chairs

The most durable accomplishment of the French during this century was the upholstered armchair —the fauteuil with open arms and the bergère with closed arms. Comfortable for both men and women, they were a good deal more graceful and lighter looking than their English counterparts.

1

The *Régence* armchair was comfortable but rather large in scale like its predecessors in the reign of Louis XIV.

2

Louis XV fauteuil retained the cabriole legs, had a broad back, but was not so high.

4

Louis XVI armchair had straight, tapered legs, usually fluted. Frame was painted pale colors or gilded. This design with oval medallion back is exceptionally popular today.

3

Transitional bergère began to be more restrained. Back was sometimes square; serpentine line of seat disappeared.

English and American Chairs

English chairs and their American derivatives were more varied in design than the French. But except for some Windsors and the Sheraton styles at the end of the century, the wood —first walnut, later mahogany— was always given a natural finish.

1

Ladder-back rush-seat chair, with or without arms, was probably the most common chair in ordinary houses both in England and the Colonies.

2

Windsor chair with scooped-out plank seat and spindle back was especially popular in modest Colonial houses.

3

Queen Anne chair with splat back and cabriole legs began as a court piece in carved walnut. But in the Colonies many were made of maple and pine.

4

Corner chair, which had first appeared in previous century, took on vase-shaped splats and cabriole legs of Queen Anne style. Chair was used mostly at desk.

5

Early Chippendale upholstered chair "in French taste" retained cabriole legs. Later version with straight legs was known as "Martha Washington" chair.

6

Chippendale side chairs with openwork back splats were often elaborately carved—especially those made in Philadelphia.

7

Ladder-back chairs with pierced horizontal rails are often called "Chippendale," though none appear in his design books.

8

"Gothic" was a term applied to Chippendale chairs with Gothic arches and quatrefoils worked into design of back splat.

9

Bamboo-turned chair, often linked with Chippendale, reached height of popularity mainly in England at end of century. It was revived with enthusiasm in the 1960s, especially for garden rooms.

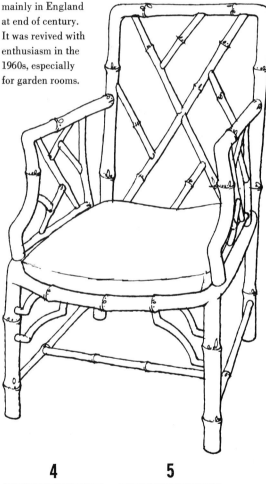

10

Shield backs enclosing balusters or splats were an earmark of the Hepplewhite style, actually an adaptation of Adam. Legs were usually straight and tapered.

11

Square backs, divided in three by a splat or balusters, were Sheraton's favorites, with the legs turned and reeded.

12

Early wing chairs had cabriole legs, claw-and-ball feet. Arm terminating in vertical roll was typical of New England and New York.

13

Hepplewhite wing chairs had deeper wings and straight, square legs. Horizontally rolled arms were popular in Philadelphia.

Sofas

As the social customs of the tea table and the salon came to have more importance, the stiff settee grew into the longer, more comfortable sofa.

1

Serpentine-back sofa in the Chippendale style reflects rolled arms of wing chair 13, *above*, and straight legs and stretchers of armchair 8.

2

Curved-back sofa in the Hepplewhite style had exposed wood on back rail and concave front of arms.

3

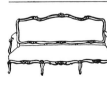

Sheraton sofa almost always had a straight back. Arms were often supported by a vase-shaped column. Legs were round, tapered and reeded.

4

Louis XV sofas were elaborately carved, closely resembled Louis XV chairs such as 2, *opposite page.*

5

Louis XVI sofas usually had straight, rectangular backs and the same straight, fluted legs as Louis XVI chair 4, *opposite page.*

Tables

During the 18th century, more and more tables were designed for special purposes, such as serving tea when that custom was brought from the Orient. Many had space-saving aspects.

1
The candle stand had a top just large enough to hold a candle, but it was tall enough to keep light at comfortable height.

2
Large drop-leaf tables with cabriole legs in Queen Anne style were used for dining, especially in houses lacking separate dining rooms.

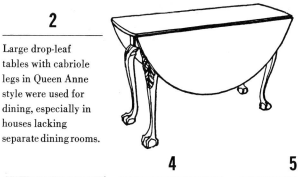

3
Queen Anne tea table often had a dished top with raised molding and, sometimes, pull-out shelves for candles.

4
Card tables, both French and English, had round or square tops hinged in center so one half could fold flat or be raised against wall.

5
Small French tables of rich wood veneers, to hold candles or urns, were popular under Louis XV.

6
Tilt-top tripod table with pie-crust edge was also used for tea, could be pushed against wall when tea was over.

7
Drop-leaf Pembroke table, often used for breakfast, came in with Hepplewhite style. Some versions had rectangular leaves and cross stretchers.

8
Louis XVI trictrac table became a reading table when the marquetry panel was raised on its easel support.

Desks and Secretaries

Furniture designed for writing became elaborately ornamental as well as functional. Chippendale launched the true secretary.

1
Block-front secretary with bonnet top was an elegant American type—specifically Newport—with no English counterpart.

2
Slant-top desk with bracket feet was very popular in the Colonies. Plain ones like this were made in Newport for export to the West Indies.

6
Bombé or kettle secretary was developed from bombé chest especially popular in Holland. Lower part swelled out at front and sides.

3
Hepplewhite tambour desk had fold-over writing surface and upper section of pigeonholes and small drawers hidden by sliding tambour doors.

7
Double pedestal desk, forerunner of our office desks, was popular in both France and England. Tops were usually covered with leather.

4
Venetian secretaries, designed along Queen Anne lines, had intricate inner fittings, were lavishly decorated with lacquer.

8
Fall-front desk or *secrétaire à abattant* was introduced in France under Louis XV. Sometimes it had a marble top, was decorated with marquetry, paint or bronze doré.

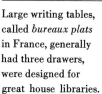

5
Large writing tables, called *bureaux plats* in France, generally had three drawers, were designed for great house libraries.

Beds

The bed achieved far more importance as decorative furniture, often dominating the room as it does today. Wooden frames replaced rope supports for bedding.

1

High-poster bed came in when houses became easier to heat. Posts supported wood frame for canopy or valance.

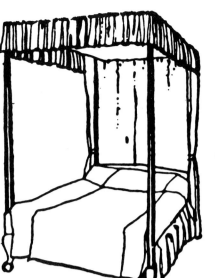

2

"Field beds" were so called because they resembled the demountable beds used when traveling.

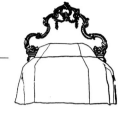

3

French alcove bed, with headboard and footboard of equal height, was popular from time of Louis XVI.

4

Venetian bed, with luxuriously carved and painted headboard, but no footboard, no hangings, prevailed in the South.

Chests of Drawers

Commodes and chests took on a great variety of shapes and heights. On the whole, they were simpler than those of the previous century.

1

Early chests of drawers were fairly undistinguished, usually stood on bracket feet. Mirror was a separate piece.

2

Philadelphia lowboy, with claw-and-ball feet and richly carved knees, is one case where American design is more ornate.

3

Louis XVI commode was marked by straight lines and straight legs, typical of neoclassical period.

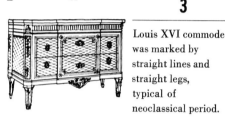

4

Block-front chests were similar to Chippendale chests, except for blocking which was unique to Colonies. Carved shell spells Newport.

5

Chest-on-chest of tallboy offered maximum storage in minimum space. Flat top and bracket feet were popular around Charleston, South Carolina.

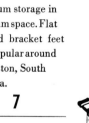

6

Hepplewhite bowfront chests had feet of flaring, French bracket type and drawers embellished with bands of light satinwood.

7

Flattop or Queen Anne highboy was earlier type and the one most popular in New England, where it was often made of maple or cherry.

8

French half-round or demilune commodes were richly decorated. Central tier of drawers was flanked by cabinets.

9

Philadelphia bonnet top highboy was probably the epitome of American Colonial cabinetmaking. It had practically no parallel among English furniture.

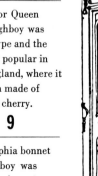

10

French provincial commodes, usually made of fruitwood in natural finish, were simplified adaptations of the Louis XV style.

Cabinets

As personal and family possessions increased, the need arose for storage designed for special purposes: clothes (there were no built-in closets), china, books.

1

Hudson River Valley *kas* was decorated with painted trompe l'oeil motifs, to simulate carving on 17th-century Dutch clothes cupboards.

2

Corner cupboards, usually intended for china, made use of space that would otherwise have gone to waste.

3

French provincial armoires furnished closet-shy country châteaus, are popular today to house stereo and bars.

4

Breakfront bookcase got its name because projecting center section "broke" line of facade. Some included a writing compartment.

19th CENTURY

Design in the 19th century was one of extremes. The classicism of the late 18th century survived wars and revolutions to find expression in the early 1800s in the Directoire and Empire styles in France, the Regency style in England and the Federal furniture of the young American republic. But by mid-century, the classic was passé. In England and America, the Gothic style was revived, and about the same time there was another revival called "Renaissance." In France, the Louis XV and XVI styles reappeared and adaptations of both combined to create Victorian rococo.

Meanwhile, design was influenced by new technical developments. In New York, John Henry Belter invented a method of bending several layers of laminated wood to form a chair back, then embellishing it with elaborate carving. In Austria, Michael Thonet invented a process of steam-bending beechwood that made possible a new kind of chair frame. The perfection of the coil spring opened the way for fully upholstered furniture with no wood visible. Finally, as power machinery—particularly saws—became more prevalent, individual craftsmanship gradually gave way to machine production.

By the beginning of the 20th century, 19th-century furniture had fallen into total disrepute. During the 1960s, however, its appeal and value in America received three important boosts: The first was the redecoration of several rooms in the White House and Blair House with furniture of the periods in which they had been furnished originally. The second was a new United States Customs ruling that redefined "antique" as anything over a hundred years old rather than anything made before 1830. The third was the superb display of 19th-century furniture among the special exhibits with which New York's Metropolitan Museum of Art celebrated its 1970 Centennial.

Although signed work by the top cabinet-makers brings high prices today, good 19th-century furniture is still available at modest prices and likely to increase in value.

Storage Cabinets

During this century, cabinets ran the gamut from ostentatious showpieces to modest but ingenious cupboards.

1

English Regency bookcases were massive in scale but comparatively simple in line—often with gilded metal mounts.

2

Shaker pie cupboard with pierced panels of tin was one of many designs that the American religious sect created to meet practical needs.

3

Gothic bookcases, like most Gothic furniture of the mid-century, were usually designed for specific houses built in the Gothic style.

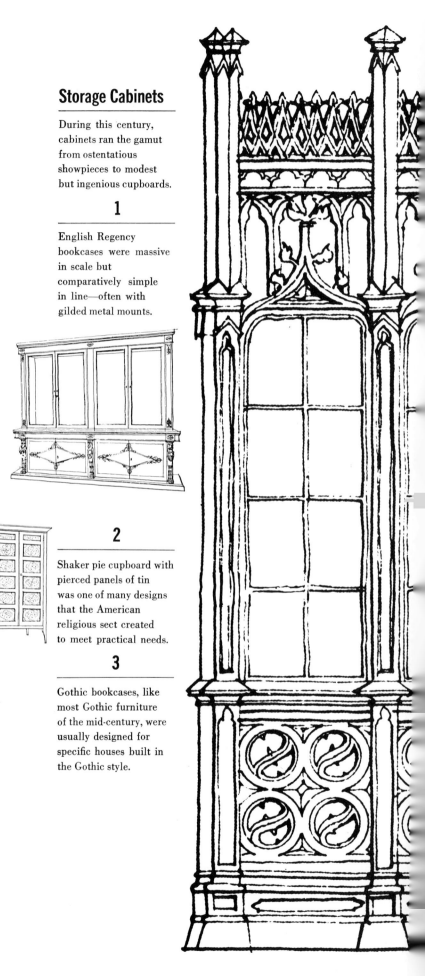

Display Cabinets

When travel became easier and the middle class more affluent, the collector was born. Whatever he collected, he wanted to display on shelves and brackets.

1

The Regency bookcase on casters was designed primarily as a portable library but was sometimes used also as a server.

2

Small American Federal cabinet for the dining room had shelves for display of china as well as drawers for silver.

3

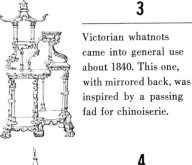

Victorian whatnots came into general use about 1840. This one, with mirrored back, was inspired by a passing fad for chinoiserie.

4

Gothic whatnot, like many designed during the 1850s, fitted into a corner, had mirrored doors.

Desks

The basic forms of desks remained for the most part unchanged, but the details followed the styles of the period.

1

French Empire writing table with characteristic metal mounts was expanded by an upper section of small drawers.

Tables

During the 19th century, several new kinds of tables emerged: the extension table designed specifically for the separate dining room; the sewing table; the sofa table to be placed in front of a sofa; the center or parlor table.

1

Duncan Phyfe's sewing tables, with chamfered corners, pedestal bases and tambour fronts, inspired adaptations for several decades.

2

Lacquered worktables with lift-up tops were prized in England and on the Continent.

3

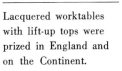

Shaker sewing cabinet was a graceful but no-nonsense design, with drop leaf in back where it would not interfere with drawers.

4

Federal card table had typical lyre supports and four Greek saber legs. Card tables were very popular through the first half of the century.

2

American Empire secretaries with simplified lines were often made in highly figured veneers of mahogany or walnut.

5

Extension dining tables took many forms. Straight legs were less common than pedestal supports set on saber legs. Sometimes ends could be used as consoles.

6

Regency console table, with marble top and scroll and lyre supports, inspired similarly ornate designs like those of Franco-American cabinetmaker Charles Honoré Lannuier.

7

Drop-leaf sofa tables gave the ladies a place to spread out their work, sometimes substituted for dining tables.

8

Drop-leaf center tables with pedestal bases and lion's-paw feet were made in America in great numbers during the 1830s.

9

Round center tables of same period were supported by a pillar or three columns set on a triangular base.

10

Belter parlor tables had marble tops and frames of carved laminated rosewood.

Beds

Slowly the high-poster bed disappeared, its place taken by heavier looking styles with fewer curtains or none.

1

French Empire bed, designed to be placed against the wall, inspired adaptations in England and America.

2

Sleigh bed of American Empire period followed same lines, was less massive.

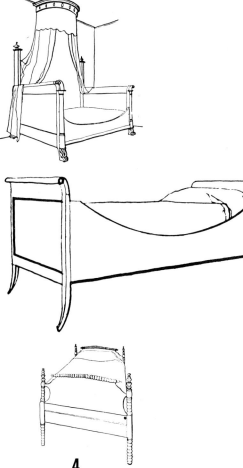

3

Renaissance revival style came in about 1850. Beds had towering headboards topped with crests.

4

Spool bed was standard in bedroom sets of painted "cottage furniture," designed from 1840 on.

Chests and Bureaus

Single chests grew taller until the introduction around mid-century of dressing-bureau, a lower but wider piece with its own mirror.

1

American Federal chest retained earmarks of Sheraton style: round columns projecting from corners, slightly bowed drawer fronts.

2

French Empire chest was taller, heavier looking, decorated with carved classic motifs.

3

American Empire chest beginning about 1835 had projecting columns at front corners to support overhanging top drawers.

4

Renaissance revival dressing-bureau was lower because marble top was used as dressing table. Mirror sometimes was attached to back, sometimes hung on wall.

5

Later Renaissance bureau was very low in center to make surface convenient for a seated woman. Mirrors gave full-length view, often reached ceiling.

Sofas

From the neoclassic forms of the early years, 19th-century sofas developed into late Victorian extravaganzas.

1

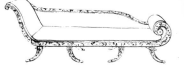

Greek couch with saber legs was a French Directoire-Empire design promptly adopted in England and America in first decade of century.

2

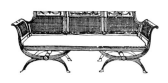

Directoire-style sofa also had a neoclassic feeling. Except for elaborate top rail, this is similar to one in the Red Room of the White House.

3

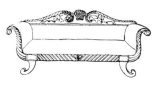

Duncan Phyfe sofa, about 1810 to 1820, had cane back and arms and X-shaped supports inspired by Roman curule bench.

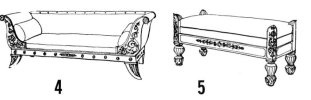

4

English Regency sofa was heavier looking and elaborately decorated.

5

Duncan Phyfe window bench of about 1820 was decorated with gold leaf.

6

Cast iron garden benches began to appear in the 1840s, often following Louis XV lines almost literally.

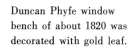

7

Medallion-back sofas of rococo or Louis XV revival period were usually covered with black horsehair, deeply channeled and tufted.

8

Ottoman or French *borne*, designed to be placed in center of room, was one of earliest forms of fully upholstered furniture.

Chairs

Some of the most successful 19th-century designs were chairs, especially side chairs which are much in demand today as accents for modern dining rooms.

1

Klismos, borrowed from chair found on Greek vases, inspired numerous adaptations in early decades of century. Original klismos had broad, overhanging back rail, saber legs.

2

Lyre-back chairs, with scroll arms and saber legs of early French Empire period, were quickly adopted by American chairmakers.

3

"Sheraton fancy chair," *far left*, referred to any lightweight chair with painted decoration and rush or cane seat. Lambert Hitchcock of Connecticut developed his own versions with stenciled decoration, *left*.

4

Shaker ladder-back, with basket-weave seat of heavy tape, was a refined version of a common country chair.

5

Boston rocker appeared in New England about 1825. A country style, it was usually painted black, then stenciled.

6

French *chaise gondole* of Charles X period (1814–1830) was later copied almost exactly in America.

7

Balloon-back came to America from England about 1840, was most important shape for side chairs until rococo style declined about 1870.

8

Rococo chairs sometimes combined Louis XVI back with Louis XV frame and legs.

9

Belter chairs were most flamboyant examples of rococo style because of spectacular carving on laminated wood backs.

10

Gentleman's chair, an adaptation of the Louis XV bergère, was an essential item of every rococo parlor set.

11

Morris chair was a product of late 19th-century ingenuity. A steel rod and ratchet behind back raised and lowered it as desired. Design is often attributed to William Morris but without much evidence.

12

Bentwood chairs, at first a whirl of curls, were later greatly simplified. Strength, lightness, resiliency and comfort kept the style alive until it was hailed as "modern" in mid-20th century. Bentwood rocker was designed about 1870.

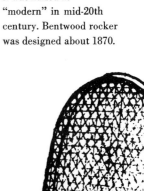

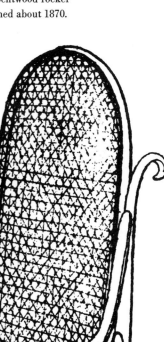

20th CENTURY

During the first seventy years of the 20th century, furniture design was a counterpoint of revival and invention—now one of them dominant, now the other. Some revivals took the form of "authentic reproductions." For the first time, exact copies rather than loose adaptations were made of the furniture designs of the past.

On the inventive side, the 20th century marked the first great flowering of American design. Although American cabinetmakers of the 18th and 19th centuries contributed importantly to the styles of their times, their designs were based originally on French and English precedents. The first wholly indigenous American style is often claimed to be Mission, derived from designs published in the magazine <u>The Craftsman</u>, and from furniture found in the old missions of California. But by the period immediately following World War II, American designers were leading the world, their closest rivals being the Scandinavians. In the sixties, however, the tremendous surge in international trade almost wiped out national boundaries. Designs from Italy (just zooming into international importance), from Denmark, Finland and other countries were not merely emulated in America but were actually exported in sizable quantities, along with American furniture, to every part of the world.

The century's most important technical development had to do with materials. Until 1925, almost all indoor residential furniture was made basically of wood. Other materials were used for decoration but rarely as part of the basic construction. Starting with the introduction of steel tubing in the twenties, however, one material after another was found feasible until, by the end of the sixties, steel, glass, and plastics of all types were accepted as logical partners for wood. Some furniture, in fact, contained no wood at all.

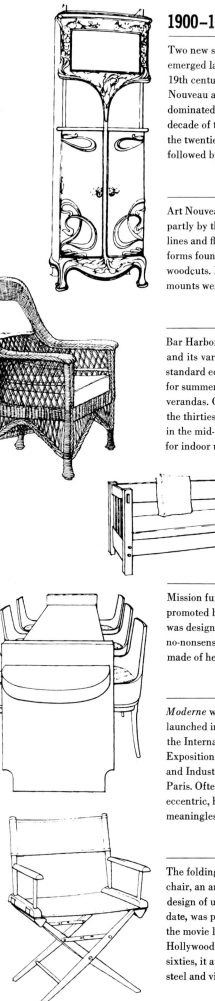

1900–1925

Two new styles that had emerged late in the 19th century—Art Nouveau and Mission—dominated the first decade of the 20th. In the twenties, they were followed by *art moderne.*

1

Art Nouveau was inspired partly by the swirling lines and flower forms found in Japanese woodcuts. Decorative mounts were of iron.

2

Bar Harbor wicker chair and its variants were standard equipment for summer house verandas. Gone by the thirties, it returned in the mid-sixties for indoor use.

3

Mission furniture, promoted by *The Craftsman,* was designed on straight, no-nonsense lines and made of heavy, fumed oak.

4

Moderne was officially launched in 1925 at the International Exposition of Decorative and Industrial Art in Paris. Often it was eccentric, had meaningless details.

5

The folding director's chair, an anonymous design of uncertain birth date, was practical on the movie lots of Hollywood. In the late sixties, it appeared in steel and vinyl.

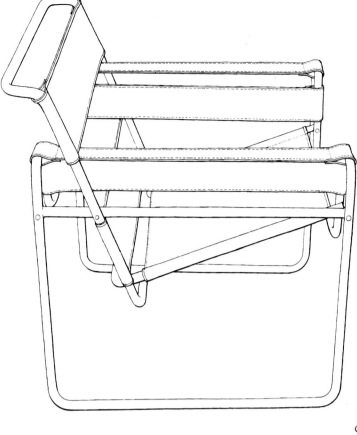

1925–1940

Modern, as we know it, began with furniture designed by architects to show what was right for the machine age. Not very popular at first, it was revived with enthusiasm some decades later.

1

"Wassily" adjustable lounge chair of tubular steel and leather was designed in 1925 by architect Marcel Breuer, then at the famous Bauhaus design school at Weimar.

2–3

Le Corbusier, a famous French architect, designed a few pieces of furniture in the twenties that were revived forty years later. In 1928 he created an armchair made of leather-covered cushions set in a frame of tubular steel, and an adjustable chaise with steel frame supported by an ebonized steel cradle.

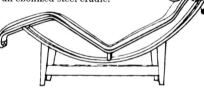

4

"Cesca" cantilevered armchair designed by Marcel Breuer in 1928 was a milestone because it introduced a resilient support of tubular steel as an alternative to legs. Although it inspired a rash of "dinette" furniture, the original was a rarity until put into production in the late sixties.

5

Cantilevered chair, designed by Finnish architect Alvar Aalto in 1935, was based on same principle, but supports consisted of continuous pieces of laminated wood.

6

Barcelona chair of steel and leather, designed by Miës van der Rohe for the Barcelona International Exhibition in 1929, was reminiscent of Greek klismos. Expensive to make, it was a collector's luxury until put back into production in the sixties.

7

Steel and glass, paired in famous coffee table that Miës designed in 1930 for the Tugendhat house, became highly fashionable thirty years later.

Post-World War II

The war and the period
of readjustment
halted the production
of newly designed
furniture until 1947.
Then came an explosion,
a proliferation of
new designs and new
systems mainly by
American designers, that
lasted well into the
fifties. Most of
these have lived
to become modern classics.

1

In Finn Juhl's chairs,
upholstered seat and
back seemed to
float within wooden frame.
His designs were
leaders of the
"Danish modern" style.

2

Charles Eames's chair of
1946 combined molded
plywood, steel rods and
rubber shock mounts
for the first time
and became a classic
almost overnight.

3

T. H. Robsjohn-Gibbings's
first postwar chair,
simple but elegant,
pointed a new design
direction for furniture
of traditional materials
and construction.

4

The Chiavari chair, an
anonymous design
made for generations in
Chiavari on the Italian
Riviera, was welcomed
here because of
its sturdy simplicity,
exceptionally low price.

5

Edward Wormley was one
of the first to slim
down upholstered
furniture. He set metal
legs in from edge
for "floating" effect.

6

George Nelson, who had
worked out the
revolutionary concept of
the storage wall as an
integral part of the
house structure, later
translated it into a
series of modular
cabinets, shelves, chests,
etc., that could be put
together like blocks.

7

Bruno Mathsson of Sweden
devised a remarkable
drop-leaf table that
could be extended
from a 9-inch sliver to
over 9 feet.

8

Eero Saarinen designed
in 1953 his "Tulip"
chair of molded fiber
glass on a cast
aluminum pedestal.
Matching tables in all
sizes had similar
bases, marble tops.

9

Charles Eames in 1956
extended his molded
plywood idea to a lounge
chair and ottoman that
were every man's
dream of comfort.

10

Harry Bertoia devised a
chair of steel wire,
sometimes upholstered
with foam rubber to
which fabric was bonded.

11

Hans Wegner's beechwood
armchair with caned
seat, a modern captain's
chair, epitomized the
style of this Danish
master cabinetmaker.

RIEGER

The 1960s

About mid-decade came a new burst of invention. Transparent plastic, long available, finally came into its own along with earlier 20th-century ideas.

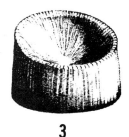

3

Mushroom lounge chair in wicker, by Finnish designer Eero Aarnio, made a good companion for wicker Bar Harbor chairs recently revived.

4

"Plug-in" storage system by George Nelson carried storage wall one step further. Shelves, chests, cabinets could be "plugged in" to poles held in spring tension, demounted later for moving.

5

"Bastiano" chair by Italian designer Tobia Scarpa—a straight-lined wood frame filled with soft cushions—recalled Le Corbusier's 1928 chair.

6

"Egg" chair by Danish designer Arne Jacobsen consisted of a molded fiber glass shell, padded with foam rubber, pivoting on a steel pedestal.

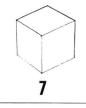

7

The cube, introduced in exotic woods by Edward Wormley, was translated into see-through plastic.

8

Parsons table with square legs set flush with top became popular in all sizes, from chairside to dining.

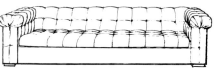

1

Deep-tufted sofa by Edward Wormley was an early example of the return to massive comfort and the "soft-edge" look.

2

Transparent plastic cocktail table by Neal Small led a long parade of see-through furniture.

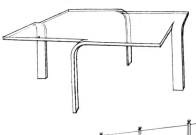

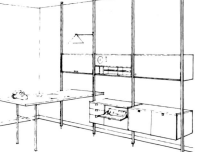

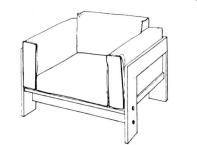

New Shapes for the Seventies

Toward the end of the sixties, new uses of new plastics led to radical changes in form that many believed heralded an entirely new kind of furniture.

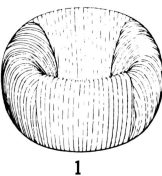

1

Spherical chair of polyurethane by Italian designer Gaetano Pesce inflates automatically when container is opened.

2

Transparent vinyl sofa by French designer Quasar Khanh can be carried home, deflated, in a shopping bag.

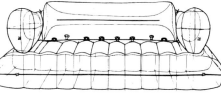

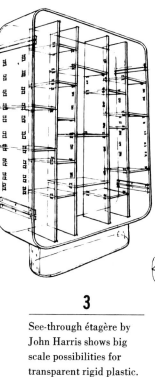

3

See-through étagère by John Harris shows big scale possibilities for transparent rigid plastic.

4

"Gyro" chair by Eero Aarnio of reinforced molded fiber glass offers new concept for lounging.

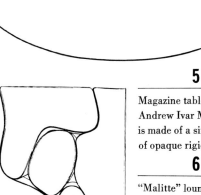

5

Magazine table, *right*, by Andrew Ivar Morrison is made of a single sheet of opaque rigid plastic.

6

"Malitte" lounge group by Italian designer Sebastian Matta consists of fabric covered polyurethane foam blocks that can be used separately, together or assembled, *above left*, to form a space divider.

Chapter 6

TALENTED ROOMS

TRIUMPHS OF
STYLE
AND
LIVABILITY

Talent that counts is a natural capacity that has been developed to its fullest. Rooms, like people, have capacities; recognize them, put them to work, and you have highly talented rooms. A soaring ceiling, for example, has a potential for excitement and a sense of liberation, but if it is ignored it can be oppressive, discomforting. A view, a fireplace, a sunny exposure, a huge floor space, a sweet small space —all these and many more are gifts that you can bring out and develop into full-blown talents. Naturally, unless you are building or remodeling extensively, the floor plan and structural elements of a room control, to some extent, its possibilities. Although your own family life style should dictate the use of your spaces, you must also listen to what the spaces tell you. If the sweet small room is decorated to the limit of its potential for intimacy —lined with fabric, perhaps, or invitingly furnished with small-scale pieces —it will resound with rightness; if you try to force it out of character with too many space-stretching de-

vices, it will balk and fail you. The ability to develop a room's decorative talents is part instinct, part experience and education. Your goal: to make a room a pleasure to look at and a delight to live in.

Talents can be functional as well as visual, however. One of the most useful and endearing talents a room can possess today is flexibility—a product of adequate space, clever dual-purpose furniture and careful planning. Gone is the era when bedrooms were only for sleeping, dining rooms only for eating around a set table, living rooms only for stage-set socializing. The living room has become a happy place where people enjoy themselves during their hours of leisure. Frequently it incorporates the dining area and settings for games, hobbies, music equipment.

Dining rooms are very apt to play dual roles and also be delightful sitting areas, much-used libraries, even occasional guest rooms. A home workshop or office is often established in a room that has a second or third func-

tion, and kitchens with charming, convenient arrangements for eating are more usual than not.

It is a simple matter to give a good-sized bedroom secondary attractions with small furniture groupings for conversation, reading, desk work, sewing, television, eating breakfast.

Another working talent in our servantless days is ease of maintenance. The room that requires a minimum of meticulous care is endlessly gratifying. Livability is a talent that you can develop in a room of any size and shape, with cooperative furniture arrangement and lighting, comfort, convenience. Efficiency is a special characteristic for which there is no substitute in hard-working areas— kitchen, laundry, storage spaces, bathrooms. None of these can serve you properly unless they are so well organized that they almost run themselves.

Not all rooms can be equally talented, nor should all of them have identical talents, but each can excel in its own ways, many of which are shown and discussed in this chapter.

Gifted in many ways, *right,* the living room of a holiday house is immensely flexible, a joy to look at and easy to look after. Every good feature is played up to the hilt. An inviting living area focuses on the fireplace; a table for games has its separate space; the dining area is superbly lighted by skylights. White curtains scarcely interrupt the magnificent view, and black-stained roof trusses dramatize a 20-foot ceiling. The handsome, mostly bare brick floor needs little care except quick sweepings.

HALLS AND STAIRS

**SMALL SPACES
WITH
BIG RESPONSIBILITIES**

A front hall is an introduction to a house and not only should welcome all comers warmly, it should also give a clue to the personality of that house. Halls other than entrance halls are important links between rooms and should connect them decoratively as well as actually. An open staircase in any hall almost invariably leads to another hall on the floor above or below, which you should consider when working out your overall scheme.

Even if an entry is very small, you can give it an inviting aura with color or pattern on the walls, a few pictures or other individual touches, an attractive (and practical) rug or hard floor covering. A mirror makes an area seem larger and is especially handy in a front hall. If possible, have at least a chair or bench in your entrance hall, and a table or chest for holding things. Of course, a large hall gives you more leeway to create a room-like quality.

Long walls are really sweeping blank canvases to be turned into visual delights with such devices as interesting wallpaper, pictures, bookshelves, if you have enough space. Stair walls—even those that enclose the narrowest steps—can always be given a lift, if only with a pretty paper or fresh color. And the stairs can be turned to decorative advantage in many ways.

Any hall scheme you choose should relate to the rooms opening off that hall. Its ambiance, colors and quality should carry a continuity of harmony from a hall through doors and into adjoining rooms.

Country delights, *right*—brick paving, flourishing plants and treillage-inspired wall covering—make an entrance hall pretty as a garden path. Furniture, too, conveys the family's love of flowers; the bench opposite the front door has needlepoint blossoms; the mirror above is crowned by garden tools. Interior design: Thomas Fleming and Keith Irvine.

Provincial treasures, *left,* in a simply furnished center hall, hint at the many charming Gallic touches to be found throughout an American Francophile's country retreat. The Louis XVI buffet is flanked by chairs convenient to both ends of a hall which runs from front to rear. Antique French prints, arrayed to complement the architecture, are set off by a soft color the owner favors for pictures. Painted "runner" on the stairs is a local custom considered safer than carpet.

BEADLE

GRIGSBY

A mélange of antiques, *left,* only a small part of an indefatigable collector's harvest, is held together in a gallery by an equally exuberant mix of hues and patterns. White ceiling, dark floors, and woodwork painted a quiet color offset the riches. Interior design: Everett Brown.

Charming provisions, *right,* by the turn of a staircase, extend a warm welcome. For comfort underfoot, a gros point carpet; for comfort in the sun, a battery of hats within easy reach; for protection, umbrellas, each gaily colored. Interior design: Mrs. Henry Parish II.

Precise snaps of color, *below,* enliven a hallway wisely kept uncluttered. Contrasting trim turns paneled doors into decorative assets and points up handsome door frames. Needlepoint rug cuts a vivid path, its length balanced by the height of a beautifully placed, tall grandfather's clock. Interior design: David Laurence Booth.

GRIGSBY

BRIGHT

GRIGSBY

Step-by-step design, *left,* leads the eye up a stone stairway to the floor above. Ceramic tiles were especially made for each riser. Lively and practical, the idea could be carried out with vinyl tiles. Interior design: Paolo D'Anna.

Crisp geometries, *above,* add a refreshing look to an entrance hall. With an adjoining coat closet and powder room papered alike, the hall offers guests all the amenities. Interior design: Angelo Donghia of Burge-Donghia.

165

YEE

Exuberant furnishings, *above,* are used with restraint in a large entrance hall. Grand in scale and worthy of admiring glances on the way to the living room are the French faience stove (10 feet high) and, catching its image, a magnificent mirror opposite. Hall's colors, however, are quiet white and beiges. Interior design: Michael Taylor.

Collection of mirrors, *left,* adds drama to a narrow strip of wall space between a window and a stairway. Each mirror, framed in *pietra dura* and ebony, reflects a portion of the scene its own way, making a fascinating composition. Interior design: Paolo D'Anna.

Multitude of pictures, *right,* covers the walls of an entrance hall in the house of dedicated art collectors. They believe paintings should be hung in a crowd so guests can enjoy the pleasure of making many discoveries. Frames ranging along the stairway are firmly fastened so they cannot be tipped.

BRIGHT

SILVA

LIVING ROOMS

THE HEART OF THE HOUSE

Everybody uses your living room—family, friends, acquaintances, strangers brought to the house for the first time. What that room says about ease, welcome, cheerfulness and warm living is what you feel yourself about all these graces of life. Almost always, a living room has the largest amount of space in a house and is allotted the biggest share of the decorating budget. What a talented place you can make it—if you develop its many possibilities! Here is the heart of the house, and the more flexibility it has, the more opportunities it can offer—for an hour of privacy at a desk or with a book, for random talk and enjoyment within the family, for intimate little parties and large, jovial gatherings. Actually, flexibility is a collection of comforts that can adapt themselves to various occasions: good seating served by good lighting; handy surfaces for magazines, ashtrays, whatever; light chairs and little tables ready to join one group or another; bookshelves within easy reach; TV within easy viewing. Given the space, areas for dining, games, drink-mixing, stretch the room's appeal. On these pages are living rooms worthy of their name.

Great sweep of space, *left,* under a swooping arch, combines the social pleasures of living, dining and cooking (view is from the open kitchen). Furnishings, mostly built-in, make the huge, highly talented room easy to care for. Dining table of polished granite is embedded in the flagstone floor; conversation pit is lined with carpet, snugged with sofas. Panes go uncurtained to play up shapes of light. For summer entertaining, glass wall opens to a terrace. Architects: Marcel Breuer and Herbert Beckhard.

A sylvan mood, *right,* fills an inviting living room whose country charms seem wide open to trees and sky. Rough beams, glass and brick give the room's contemporary architecture an ageless quality. In harmony are the warm reds repeated numerous ways, and the restrained designs of the wood furniture. By day, plastic-domed skylights lift the view; after dark, the focus shifts to the raised hearth.

Serene surroundings, *below*, for quiet talk, small gatherings or large parties, are created with many neutrals, varied textures, quiet patterns. Walls and sofas are striped in beige; chairs add dark accents. For luster: a smoked mirrored screen, a steel and glass table. To ease party traffic, a tiny coffee table by one sofa frees floor space. Interior design: Paul M. Jones.

MAYA

Playful atmosphere, *left*, pervades the many-faceted room for a lively family. Making blithe use of the middle space is a mahogany swing—vast perch for loungers, cozy roost when turned in winter to hang facing the hearth. The other furniture is so simple that it in no way distracts from the excitement of paintings and sculpture. To keep the room high-spirited, shelf edges are a vivid maze of color, and wall panels are frequently repainted in contrasting hues.

YEE

TALENTED ROOMS
LIVING ROOMS

Nostalgic appeal, *above*, of a remodeled barn, gives a particular warmth to
easy-going gatherings, and to a medley of old treasures, contemporary furniture,
fascinating sculpture. The various wood tones of beams and furnishings get a
wallop from reds. They show up in many contrasting shapes—in a curvaceous chair,
the big painting of a seed packet, masses of flowers. Clearly defined traffic lanes
subtly direct circulation and steer party crowds to a nearby dining room and terrace.

Elegant aura, *right*, is evoked in a small but lofty room that boasts two focal
points—a fireplace and a handsome bay. To magnetize attention: The hearth is
given added importance by a superb mirror, and the bay's garden vistas are framed
with black and left curtain-free. The damask-covered sofa takes in both
major attractions and echoes the yellow of the walls. Interior design: Barton L. Davis.

**TALENTED ROOMS
LIVING ROOMS**

Sharp definition, *above,* of contemporary furnishings, makes an old-fashioned room look as new as tomorrow. Changing the size of the conversation groups is easy—with pull-up chairs, a couple of sofas, two sleek coffee tables and plenty of open space. Holding all together: a geometrically patterned rug. Wall moldings are painted out, so attention goes to the play of leather, chrome and gleaming plastics. Interior design: Alain Lariviere.

Distinct division, *right,* of one large, inviting room into three areas, is accomplished by wise furniture arrangement. At one end, a dining table and green-lacquered chairs stand on the bare floor. A seating group in the center takes in a terrace view. Love seat backed by a table-desk flanks the fireplace. Relating all parts are bright flowers in frames and printed on fabrics, leaf greens, wood browns. Interior design: Thomas Fleming, Keith Irvine.

DINING ROOMS

Today's dining rooms are versatile, full of surprises, livelier than ever. Many of them serve some other purpose between meals, but whether they do or not, they are warmer, more friendly for family meals and hospitable for entertaining. Gone is the formidable assemblage of dark-finished furniture, the rigidity, the solemnity. Light woods, caning, brightly painted or upholstered chairs, patterns, paintings, all spark the dining scene. Contemporary tables are often teamed with traditional chairs or vice versa. And where tradition dominates, it does so with a new sprightliness.

Our way of life and entertaining today is so many-faceted, so rarely smoothed by good service, that a dining room should be capable of meeting any situation with aplomb. Whether the children have friends for lunch or you give a sit-down buffet supper for eight or a formal dinner for twelve, your dining room should be able to fall in with your plans, with a minimum of effort on your part. Table appointments should be stored in the room or handy to it. You should have some surface other than the table itself on which to arrange a buffet meal if you want your guests to gather around an attractively set table in comfort. Flooring that is easily cleaned or a rug that doesn't show up every spot is essential if you have children. Enough space for circulation is important when you have a crowd for cocktails or other good-sized party.

Even if your dining room is not specifically furnished to perform a second function, it can be turned to good use for games, work or other activity that requires plenty of table space. If you create an inviting setting, it will inevitably become a versatile one.

Room for parties and paintings, *left:* In a sleek setting equally suited to small or large dinner and buffet parties, a table that expands to seat sixteen dominates the center, companioned by classic contemporary chairs of tubular steel, ebony and cane. A large painting holds the room's one great rollick of color. It is balanced by bone-white surroundings, steel, and ash burl, an intricately grained wood the color of amber. The lengthy sideboard, a haven for storage, has a marble top—fine for a buffet. Making the jump from vast to tiny: bibelots on a 19th-century Biedermeier sewing stand that is shaped like the eye of a giant needle. Interior design: Armand Bartos.

GRIGSBY

Garden brightness, *below,* turns part of a remodeled city brownstone into a patio-like room as convivial for casual get-togethers as for dining. One glass wall captures year-round delights of a back garden. Facing it, an étagère—much like a tiny greenhouse—fills a doorway no longer needed as a passage. Above, a skylight in a sky-blue ceiling lets light into rooms on both sides of the étagère. Placing the table and chairs away from the center contributes to the room's courtyard role and makes access to the garden easy.

Space-age luster, *right,* of a patent leather vinyl, gives a gleaming look to a highly dramatic dining room, making it one of today's exciting new breed. Stripes cover the walls and zebra around the slope of the tray ceiling on which the gloss doubles the chandelier's glitter. A vinyl-covered screen takes the place of curtains, allows stripes to continue uninterrupted. Around a contemporary table of burled elm, white-lacquered Chippendale chairs strike a pleasing and conspicuously traditional note. Interior design: Melvin Dwork.

YEE

ECKERT

GRIGSBY

French provincial furniture, *left,* ample in
scale, suggests generous hospitality. Chairs
covered front and back in different fabrics—a
favored French custom, years ago—bring needed color into
the center of the dining room, as does the rug.
Chairs flanking an armoire introduce another
pattern. Surprise on a nearby wall: a contemporary painting.

Rural touches, *right,* and an easy mix of the old and
new, induce family and friends to linger after meals.
Slate paves the floor; dark-stained wood frames
a window kept bare so sunlight and view are unfettered.
Closet at right keeps a horde of beautiful
and amusing things for making blithely varied centerpieces.

Pattern and imagination, *left, below,* make a
multi-purpose room delightful for dining, talking,
entertaining. A small table at one end can be
used for games, little dinners or, augmented by other
tables, large parties. Sunny walls give extra
bite to black and white patterns. A bold
print stretched on frames hangs in the windows like
pictures; frames can be moved up or down as the sun dictates.

Natural tones, *below,* and natural materials play up
the unaffected charm of a very simple dining room
that can double as a workroom. Waxing brings out the
grain of a natural fir plywood tabletop; a tiny but boldly
modeled fireplace strikes a warm note in an otherwise
austere setting; an uncurtained window frames a fine view.

KORAB

YEE

GRIGSBY

LEONARD

Flowered stripes, *above*, and landscape colors merge
cheerfully in a dining room that sees
lighthearted family use during the day, more
conventional hospitality at night. Laced with white and
sunlight, many bright hues enliven the room—the
orange of vinyl cushions, blues and greens of the
over-mantel mural and the lavabo, the yellows of flowers,
real and printed. Adding to the light look: a
crystal chandelier, white chairs and the bright bare floor.

A color explosion, *right*, underfoot, on walls and on
furniture, too, brings a fresh look to a
country dining room furnished mostly with antiques
and traditional patterns and accessories. Impact
comes also from the bold design on the floor and the
pure white of the contemporary table. Woodwork
painted the warm background color of rug and wall
covering unites the two. A niche fitted with shelves
above a sideboard takes over the role of a country hutch.

KITCHENS
CENTERS THAT CATER TO CREATIVITY

The kitchen has become more fun because people enjoy being in it more. For many, cooking is now a form of personal, adventurous expression; for others, preparing meals is simply a breeze, since so many irksome chores no longer exist. As a result, today's kitchen reflects the cooking philosophy of the person who reigns there. A kitchen can be a studio for one, a bailiwick where two can work happily, or a family gathering place.

Often, a central work-and-storage island—our great advance over the old-time kitchen table—contributes enormously to the room's efficiency. If the kitchen is actually a multi-use room, the total space can be divided, without any confining partitions, into areas for meal preparation, eating, children's play, whatever. Frequently the divider is counter-high, with storage plotted to serve both sides of the room.

Whatever the plan of your kitchen, you can now put into it almost anything you like. Such limitations as *kitchen* chairs and *kitchen* curtains are obsolete. With an exhaust fan to keep everything virtually unsullied by grease, almost any colors and furnishings are as much at home in the kitchen as in any other room. So exercise your inventiveness and make your kitchen functional, amiable and personal.

Color surprise, *left:* Great blocks of red, black and white against a midnight blue wall are organized like an abstract painting, in a kitchen installed in what had been the library of a city brownstone. All major elements—from black upper cabinets to the red range—perform visually as well as functionally. This concept of total design plus easily maintained materials help a well-equipped kitchen stay young with style.

Pattern power, *right:* In a hard-working kitchen, a crisp wallpaper design turns a cooking and serving island into a decorative, eye-catching splash. Concentrating a pleasing pattern below and above eye level (see the ceiling beam), while keeping walls plain, adds cheer without confusion.

YEE

Storage kingdom, *left, above,* and *below:* A trailblazing kitchen is built around a series of lockers —quite unlike conventional cabinets—that flank an island work center. Each locker has its own combination of U-shaped and straight shelves and rods, arranged so every inch of space is used without stacking. Everything is in front— no reaching for things you can't see.

On the range side, lockers for dry and canned foods and cooking utensils are color-cued red. Behind sink and dishwasher, blue lockers hold glass, china, silver. Deep closets lined in distinctive yellow house small appliances and a food preparation center. Surfaces are covered in Formica. When the kitchen is at rest, folding doors close to make the room serene.

**TALENTED ROOMS
KITCHENS**

YEE

TALENTED ROOMS
KITCHENS:
COMPACT EFFICIENCY

A highly cooperative kitchen can be fitted into a surprisingly small space and save you many steps, but not if you have to cross the floor dozens of times in the course of preparing a meal. So make sure that appliances, cooking utensils and food preparation area are logically located. The two essentials most difficult to fit in are adequate storage and enough work surface. Open or closed storage or both can be aligned low on the floor or up on the walls, but note that out-of-reach shelves should be reserved for rarely used items, and that cupboard doors need swing-out space. Work counters can be augmented by pull-out extensions or drop-down ones hinged to a wall or door. Luckily, however, there is room in the smallest kitchen for color, pattern and a big dollop of personality.

Tiger-bright pattern, *right,* and strong geometrics have a surprising way of making a small room seem larger. Bamboo screens, looped to foil a too-high ceiling, clinch the jungle theme. To save space, base cabinets have sliding panels. Interior design: Marjorie Borradaile Helsel.

Favorite aids, *below,* of a dedicated chef-at-home, are handily arrayed out in the open. Taking no extra space yet filling the room with joy are yellow on most surfaces, red on the chairs, and both colors in the flowered curtains.

YEE

MASSEY

YEE

MARGERIN   MARIS

Paisley splash, *above,* of a decidedly non-kitcheny paper, even glorifies a storage niche made from the upper part of an unnecessary doorway. Blocking the door made it possible to add an all-important counter and base cabinets. On the end wall, a plug-in center for small appliances. Interior design: Robert Caigan.

Natural beauty, *right, top,* of lush greenery outside, and flowers and foods inside, seems extra fresh with all-white surroundings. Uncurtained window walls add a sense of spaciousness that belies the kitchen's 7-by-11-foot size.

Pass-through partition, *right, center,* of walnut cabinets, looks like built-in furniture from the dining room side and keeps the slice of kitchen from seeming too confining. Architects: Richard and Judith York Newman.

Provincial flair, *right, bottom,* adds warmth to a narrow cooking center that has little room for frills. Country touches start with ceiling beams, go on to include plant railings above the wall-hung storage units, wood window trim and paneled cabinets in a fruitwood finish. Contemporary appliances and counters are white.

BEADLE

Myriad treasures, *above,* of all kinds—a variety of beloved bibelots and unusual paintings—are lavished on a compact kitchen as they are everywhere in a collector's apartment. Variations of red spice the white. Interior design: Bonnie Cashin.

An isolated cook is a lonely cook, but lower or remove any barrier that shuts off the work center from an area where family and friends can gather, and the cook becomes one of the group. A nearby dining table and chairs will promote games and talk between meals. If space permits, add upholstered chairs for real lounging, possibly a desk, a bookcase, a setup for mixing drinks. Open up your kitchen to give it a sociable outlook, and you will open up many hours of your day.

BAER

Creating with space, *above,* turns two small rooms and a tiny front deck into a kitchen-café-family room more delightful than separated little areas. A serving and preparation counter replaces a wall between the two rooms, and a new French door leads to the charming outdoor annex. The work center, *right,* is attractive for cook and visitors alike. Mexican tin lanterns shade hanging lights, and an Oriental rug—great disguiser of stains—adds warmth underfoot. Interior design: Peter Rocchia.

Planning with zest, *far right,* gives a little kitchen-dining room the fresh look of spontaneity. Since cabinets are few, a raft of utensils and supplies are stored in plain sight, organized in pretty containers—staples in glass jars on the windowsill, liquor bottles in a basket, bar accouterments on a lacquered tray. For extra zip: a vividly patterned wallpaper high and low. Interior design: Bill Goldsmith.

BAER

Above: Old cologne bottles, relabeled, hold vinegar, oil. In the huge bottle, leftover wine turns to vinegar.

TALENTED ROOMS
KITCHENS:
PERSONAL FLOURISHES

You owe it to yourself to have a kitchen that is as personal and fun to be in as any other room in your house. Don't hesitate to gloss function with charm. Decorative things you love deserve a place in your kitchen, where you can savor them while you work. If they are also useful, such as plates, molds and trivets, so much the better. You can embellish walls without cluttering up work surfaces. Essentials such as a ventilating hood, chairs, jars for staples, need lose none of their efficiency by being attractive. Here: A sheaf of ideas to kindle your imagination, open your eyes and point the way toward sparking your kitchen.

Opposite: Imagination turns an old-time kitchen with white-tiled walls into a charming place. A brass chandelier gives a touch of grandeur; fluted borders on the stainless steel hood are pure whimsy. The quaint milking stool, a wall arrangement of favorite finds, and a chair painted to look like a basket of daisies work wonders without getting in the way. Interior design: Evelyn Jablow.

Above: Wrought iron copy of a butcher's rack shows off bright array of pans.

Above: Copper pots and pans hang on sturdy iron hooks, making a decorative point in a corner where wall cabinets would cut off lots of light from the window.

Left: A wicker bull mask, necklaced with a festoon of garlic, plus a prized painting hang over the generous range in the kitchen of a hobbyist cook.

Above: Primitive family portraits watch over a high, well-stocked shelf that also unites the pictures of various sizes.

Below: Small old cabinets, tools and a tiny painting compose a bit of scenery above a long counter in a minute space.

Above: Cache in an inaccessible cabinet corner holds liquor. Bottles are fished out from the top.

LEONARD

A laundry room, like a kitchen, should be a happy place, pretty and proficient, that does most of the work for you but makes you feel that you accomplish miracles on your own. Steam, toil and basement gloom are out. Lightness, brightness and convenience are in. Today's appliances are so trim that your laundry can go into a mere parcel of space almost anywhere—next to the kitchen, handy to bedrooms, en route to a bathroom. Little is required to give this work center a lift: gay color or pattern on floor and walls, brightly painted cabinets, good lighting. If space permits, stretch it to include areas for sewing and other pursuits you enjoy.

Multiple facilities, *above,* in a laundry, make it a pleasant place to mend clothing, write letters, arrange flowers. Along one side: sleek lineup of washer, dryer and sink. Across one end: a work counter built low for a sewing machine and typewriter. Flowered vinyl covers the walls and skylighted ceiling.

Second-floor location, *right,* gives a laundry proximity to bedrooms, helps lure each member of the family to deposit his own soiled clothes and sheets in a large, tip-out hamper. Closets provide temporary storage for clean clothes. Fruit-patterned wallpaper and a curtained window echo the decorative gaiety of nearby bedrooms. Interior design: Katherine Godwin, Inc.

GUERRERO

Fine cabinetwork, *left,* of paneled walnut, helps create a new look in a laundry. Extra-slim cabinets joined by a wood cornice frame the window. Flowered curtains and matching wallpaper abet the room's non-sterile impression. Closet is for clean clothing. Interior design: Renny B. Saltzman.

Flowered arch, *left, below,* of curtains plus mimosa-colored equipment and nylon carpeting, make a pretty sight of a laundry in a family room, even when hideaway doors are open. Carpet is the kind designed to shrug off mishaps.

Elegant touch, *right, top,* for a laundry, is provided by floor-length curtains, the sole nonworking, not absolutely necessary, element in sight. The panels of heavy cotton are banded in blue, the one color accent in an all-white room. Interior design: Noel F. Birns.

Welcoming color, *far right, top,* the brightest of oranges on undercounter cabinets and in a plaid window shade, enlivens a white laundry often used as a shortcut by family and close friends en route from the carport. Interior design: Lucille Gardner.

Spirited twin, *right,* of an adjoining kitchen, a trim laundry has sunny yellow cabinets that match those next door, and give a needed lift to the cool, north-lighted room. Equipment at right of sink is white, as is the pinup board for children's art work. On handy open shelves, fresh towels await pickup. Interior design: Charles Pollock.

Colorful parade, *far right,* of bold blue, persimmon, light blue and avocado on the sliding doors of closets, plus more strong blue on the floor, adds zip to a white laundry. The room doubles as a storage center for out-of-season clothes. Architect: Paul Edward Tay.

GUERRERO

ECKERT

ECKERT

ECKERT

ECKERT

GARDEN ROOMS

THE LURE OF THE OUTDOORS INSIDE

The garden room reflects America's love of the outdoors and our refreshingly unserious brand of decorating. The now version of the Victorian morning room and the old-time sun porch, today's garden room is sheltered but visually unconfined and marvelously flexible. It incorporates the open feeling of a terrace, the serenity of a lanai, the practicality of a family room. Filled with flowers, plants, small trees, ease-inviting furniture and beautiful views, the garden room is a charming spot for entertaining a few friends for lunch, the place where a family gathers at any hour or a lively setting for a party. The room's sunny spirit is a feat of ingenuity and, often, of technology. A garden room may evolve from remodeling (walling in a porch, roofing a terrace) or building from scratch. Often, walls are mostly glass panels that slide back to welcome fresh air or shut tight against winter's chill. Floors are usually stalwart, carefree—slate, brick, tile. Furnishings suggest outdoor colors, green leaves, blue sky and white clouds and are often sparked with accents that match garden flowers in intensity. One of the principal charms of the garden room is its refusal to be stereotyped. Give it casual or more lavish appeal; furnish it with wicker, antiques, found pieces. While bowing to no particular style, you can achieve an engaging contemporary ambiance. A garden room, like a garden, can be "a lovesome thing," but with an advantage: the room can be enjoyed rain or shine, night or day. It cleverly combines the best of two worlds.

MASSEY

Breezy hammock, *above,* piled with pillows and swinging lazily by a sunny window, brings the backyard indoors—
even into a city apartment where the garden is solely potted plants. Completing the relaxed atmosphere: bare
windows, cane chairs and, for a few moments, not a care in the world.

Marigold colors, *right,* and billowy white say summer in a room dedicated to carefree delights. Awning stripes painted overhead are repeated on cushions lining a settee. The same bright color plus white paint unites old wicker furniture and directors' chairs. Shiny, white and practical: a vinyl table cover that goes to the floor. Blithe and fresh: broccoli for a centerpiece. Interior design: Russell Norris.

MASSEY

Treillage, *left,* delightfully lacy, newly practical, creates a romantic
environment—and a protected one. The latticework is plastic,
rugged yet flexible enough to bend; and clear plastic is
laid over it, enclosing without destroying the illusion of
rooflessness. Fruits, flowers and greens—real, printed,
ceramic—add summery refreshment to a setting which, thanks to
the magic of treillage, seems much larger than its true dimensions.

Mirage, *below,* of a cool stretch of beach and sea, is actually a
painted mural that gives a glass-fronted room a second
view of summer. A trellis of painted wood, designed to
stretch the perspective, is set flush against the fool-the-eye scene.

GRIGSBY

LEONARD

GRIGSBY

Lighthearted palette, *above,* gives a decorative lilt to a mixture of ease-inducing furniture in a leafy, flowery, light-filled room. Wicker chairs are teamed with tables of traditional Chinese design, a deep-cushioned sofa, lacy chairs of wrought iron. Almost everything is covered with a blossomy fabric, but the windows are left bare to bring in sky-wide views.

Sparkling white, *left,* makes a garden room appear as light as sea foam. The delicate look is deceptive since the tile floor and linen slipcovers are eminently washable. Soda fountain and bar in the niche make this a family center, so decorative touches are on or near walls to free floor space.

Cooling blue, *right,* and nothing more, frames a lovely vista of lawn and trees, to emphasize a garden room's close kinship with nature. The glass-enclosed haven also owes its charm and soft look to a blue-and-white scheme (always refreshing) and the flowered design of the rug (a pleasant year-round stand-in for real bouquets). Interior design: McMillen, Inc.

FENN

BEADLE

Lean-to, *left,* prefabricated of glass and aluminum, replaces a poky window and thereby turns a confined place into a garden room. The little greenhouse works as a whole series of wonders: encourages green-thumbed activities, expands the visual size of the room because of the increase in light, and makes a sunny spot for breakfasting. Brick floor and old cypress barn siding set off splashes of yellow (such as the lavabo's whimsical mound of lemons). Interior design: William Cecil.

Splurge, *right,* of greenery and flowers, makes almost all the color in a white garden room alive and growing. To help build the outdoor feeling and daydream mood: a flowered chintz, chaises for lazing and a golden aviary. Interior design: Diane Tate and Marian Hall.

Pickup, *left, below,* of white plus natural sunlight and flowering plants, turns a windowed corner into a garden room and makes a delightful dining place. White paint helps very different elements to be compatible—the brick floor, wood table base, intricately carved chairs and settee from the East. For whimsy: a long-legged metal bird. Interior design: Joseph Braswell.

BEDROOMS

SERENE SANCTUMS AROUND THE CLOCK

A bedroom's primary responsibility is to the person or persons who occupy it. It is a retiring room in much more than the sleeping sense, for here is where we should be able to find serenity and privacy at any hour. Few of us have the space for a personal sitting room, but most of us can plan our bedrooms to include inviting arrangements for such pleasures as quiet conversations, reading, needlework, writing letters, listening to music, watching TV, having tea or a light meal far from any household confusion. Yet on the other hand, shutting the door, switching off the phone and cultivating the art of doing nothing is something else a satisfying bedroom should invite. When you decide on color, pattern and period, forget rules and do what delights you. But when you consider comfort and convenience, remember every detail. Your bed or beds should be excellent; only you can decide upon the right size and firmness. Bedside lights should be strong enough to read by without strain, with a switch so near at hand that you do not have to reach for it. Soft floor covering or a bedside rug is a must for making the first step out of bed a pleasant one. Total control over daylight is something most sleepers need; so is control of noise if you are fortunate enough to have a say in the matter.

Terraced haven, *left:* A versatile bedroom's ceiling-to-floor windows slide open to a luxuriantly planted parterre. A desk takes in the view, and a sitting area takes in the fireplace. The simple background is serene for sleeping, and a quiet foil for the gros point rug, painted Italian bed and vivid blue accents. Needlework spirals on the canopy and cover imitate those of the posts. Interior design: Lydia Beckwith Lee.

Inner world, *right:* Under the timbers of a remodeled barn, a spacious master bedroom has all the conveniences of a second living room—books, music, desk, chairs for relaxing. Rich in color and personality, the generous space is also flooded with daylight.

YEE

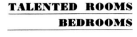

LEE

LEE

A hush of soft fabrics, *above, left,* and *right,* beautifully suits a combination of bedroom-sitting room, library-study. Every inch of the walls is upholstered in herringbone tweed—nubby, sound-deadening—outlined with glinting brass moldings. And every inch of the floor is carpeted in a crisp, non-directional pattern. Total coverage underfoot eliminates any sense of bareness in a room purposely kept simple for serenity's sake. In the reading-writing area, *above,* one wall is spanned by stout bookshelves and served by library steps that, turned about, double as an easel. Glove leather upholsters the love seat and chairs, *left,* opposite the book wall. Dominating the whole room is the very modern four-poster, *right,* that stands in an ell. Made of iron pipe railings polished to a pewter gleam, it is trimmed, like the walls, with brass. For textural contrast, bedside tables are covered in a fine French tapestry; the window shade is crocheted cotton. A detail worth noting: All lamps are identical, their shapely contours emphasized by the plainness of the walls. Interior design: John Dickinson.

TALENTED ROOMS
BEDROOMS

LEONARD

A smile of patterns, *left,* routs all obsolescence from a turn-of-the-century house. The design excitement goes right up to the ceiling and across it. High curtain tiebacks reveal window mullions. The chaise longue is covered in the same fabric as the window alcove and bedspreads but in a cooler palette. White woodwork, floor and dressing table play up shining brass beds and clothes rack. Interior design: Zajac & Callahan.

Unmatched four-posters, *right, top,* inspired the building of a bedroom-sitting room commodious enough to hold both cherished heirlooms side by side. The nonidentical designs are made harmonious by matching testers, spreads and skirts. The bay window, highly dramatic in scale, makes a scenic place for writing or for enjoying breakfast in the sun.

BEADLE

Ruffled canopy, *right,* much like a parasol, tops a Colonial brass bed, the ornate center of attraction in a guest room that has no architectural frills. The tulip-strewn fabric of the canopy and spread also covers upholstered furniture in a sitting group at the foot of the bed.

MASSEY

Splashy color, *left* and *below,* backed up by sweeps of white, changes a formerly dark place into a highly refreshing bedroom with sitting-room attractions. White gives the color extra tang, enhances views of hearth and hill, and rejuvenates old chairs. Vinyl upholstery and travertine-textured vinyl floor tiles are easy to maintain. Almost all of the master bedroom's vivid hues come from printed no-iron sheets that were used to recover ready-made quilts. The comforters ease bed-making and are practical for children to sit on. Above a built-in desk, *left,* a mirrored wall makes the room look larger.

Black and white, *right,* in two quite different patterns —a feathery print on wallpaper and a bold geometric on cotton— add up, surprisingly enough, to a tranquil atmosphere, due in large part to the absence of any distracting color. For softness: delicate undercurtains, to the floor. For sparkle: a stainless steel étagère. Helping to turn the soothing room into a bedroom-plus is an adjustable stand of chrome and acrylic. Tilted in front of a chair, the versatile piece acts as an easel for support of a book; flat, it is a tea table; raised, it is ideal for breakfast in bed. Interior design: Pengally-Winkler.

MASSEY

GRIGSBY

BEDROOMS:
FULL-TIME GUEST ROOMS

GUEST ROOM CHECK LIST

No matter how many heartfelt words of welcome you speak, your guest room can say it better. The French call the guest room the "chambre d'amis" —the friends' room—and a family is truly fortunate today if they can set aside a special room to accommodate overnight visitors.

When a guest room is sacrosanct to that purpose, steps should be taken so that it does not seem musty, unused and just-opened for the arrival. This means that a guest must find freshness: sweet air, clean surfaces, fresh linens, and curtains and flowers. Choosing fabrics for curtains and spreads that will not wilt while waiting is one tip to follow when you decorate. While there is no denying that household castoffs often find their way into guest rooms, clever use of pattern and paint can bring them up to date and tie them together visually. In addition to guide lines for freshness and comfort (see our check list, *right*), your personality is the essential factor. This is your room in your house for your relatives and friends, and there is no better compliment than to make this

room reflect your spirit. Since it is a place for short stays, you can indulge your fondness for styles that might not suit you on an everyday basis, like a saturation of red, like super-Victorian, like silvery, plastic-y slickness. People will enjoy leaving their safe beige bedrooms for a holiday in your brightly bedecked haven.

Ideally, the heads of the family should spend a night in their guest room to test its facilities. At least try napping on the beds. We use bed in the plural because twin beds are far more versatile for guest rooms than one of double size. Some couples prefer separate beds, and you may also find yourself housing a parent and child, siblings, or school friends. If you do not spend the night there, sample the light at dawn to see whether the window treatment controls it adequately. Some people wake with the first light and loss of sleep can ruin their visit. Two more tips: Insist that the children be quiet in the morning until guests are up and about. Also rule that the guest room is off premises for children unless they are asked to enter.

Beds: As comfortable as your own. Pretty linens. Good pillows, blankets. *Additional furnishings:* Bedside tables big enough for books, tissues, miscellany. A place to write notes (including paper and pen). One or two soft chairs. Full-length mirror. Luggage stands. Sizable wastebasket. *Floor covering:* At least area or scatter rugs right beside the beds. *Windows:* Operable for fresh-air addicts. Light-proof shades or curtains. *Heating:* Units that work well, quietly. *Lighting:* Gentle, general illumination plus practical concentrated light for reading in bed and for grooming. *Storage:* Adequate, sweet-smelling closet and drawer space. Hangers (not wire) for skirts, women's clothes, men's suits. Efficient clothes brush. *Bathroom amenities:* In a shared bathroom, a cleared shelf for toiletries and a rod for towels. In any bathroom guests use: new toothbrushes, toothpaste, shower cap, razor blades, shaving cream, detergent for hand washables, toilet soap, bath powder. Extra toilet and facial tissue (not hidden away). Aspirin. Sun lotion.

GRIGSBY

Inviting haven, *right,* has everything to make guests feel welcome: chaise longue complete with many pillows and a soft throw; easy chairs; well-lit dressing table and smaller tables where they are most needed. One delicately patterned print unites every part of the room—a simple device that has an extravagant effect. Roll-up, translucent blinds and light-darkening shades supplement the curtains at the many windows. Ornate details: spiral bedposts, mirror frame. Interior design: Michael Taylor.

Exuberant setting, *left,* for a weekend holiday, delights all comers with its spirited colors, a lively print, an old-time dressing table. The guest room also offers the ease of body and mind that comes when furnishings have been chosen for comfort and simple upkeep. Bamboo-turned luggage racks are permanent foot-of-the-bed furniture. Interior design: McMillen, Inc.

LYON

TALENTED ROOMS
BEDROOMS:
PART-TIME GUEST ROOMS

When a room can serve the family in one way most of the time yet gracefully extend its hospitality to a guest or two some of the time, it is exercising the talent of flexibility to the utmost. A family room, studio or study, library, relinquished domain of a grown child who does not want to say an irrevocable good-bye, or any other room that is cheerful and livable could be elected for expanded usefulness. What will enable it to double as a guest room is a comfortable bed or two (perhaps a convertible sofa, perhaps daybeds), a place where the visitor can stash his clothing—drawer space plus closet space or at least some handsome hooks on the wall for hangers—and certain minimal necessities: shades or curtains that shut out daylight; a table at the head of the bed or one that can be moved easily; a light for reading in bed that a guest can switch off without getting up.

A family study, *above,* gives no evidence by day of its bedroom potential. At night, the Empire trundle bed is made up, a desk lamp provides reading light, a pull-up table serves at the bedside. Opaque curtains and a shade keep out morning sun. Interior design: Rhoda Bright.

Unexpected quarters, *above,* for a guest is a dressing room handy to the swimming pool of a weekend house. Blithely combined for charm and surprise are French Empire furniture, a colorful toile print and a rough stone wall. Interior design: Charles Dear.

Daughter's domain, *below,* serves as a guest room when she is away at school. Armoire, *bottom,* holds all comforts for guests, including drawers, bedding, books, beauty aids and a television set. Interior design: Valerian Rybar.

Downstairs studio, *above,* in a country house, doubles as a cool-looking bedroom that is ideal for two guests. During waking hours, beds serve as couches; panels of a bamboo screen fixed to the wall act as backboards for pillows. No-fuss cotton bedspreads and vinyl floor make the living easy. Vivid paintings add swack.

Sitting room, *below,* with its quiet, sophisticated mélange of neutral colors, antiques and modern wicker, eminently suits a bachelor guest. Moldings outlining the wall panels, often considered regrettable details, are boldly painted to be crisp accents.

BATHROOMS
PRIVATE SPAS TO PAMPER YOU

The bathroom is fast becoming one of the most individual and colorful rooms in the house. It has cast off its assembly-line sterility and acquired an unmistakable bloom and vitality. Part of this is due to our new attitude toward the bath (actually a revival of the ancient Roman point of view). But just as important is the availability of imaginative floor and wall coverings that defy steam and dampness, of bright fixtures, towels, shower curtains and other delights that function no less effectively because they are wonderful to look at. Even a few towels in a smashing pattern or surprising combination of solid colors, one or two good-looking pictures on the wall and a pretty jar or two can work wonders for a stolid bathroom. More elaborately, marble, slate, terrazzo, tiles, water-resistant wallpaper, rainbow-hued fixtures (not necessarily all matching), such sybaritic installations as a sunken tub, a sauna, a whirlpool mechanism, a free-standing lavatory, together with easy chairs, rugs, plants, can give a bathroom not only unique style and personality but also health-promoting benefits that once were available only at special clubs or well-known spas.

A certain amount of self-indulgence can be very beneficial, and nowhere does it work its rejuvenating magic better than in a bathroom that caters to your own whims and taste—as well as to your basic needs.

Refreshing atmosphere, *above,* is ingeniously created with materials not usually considered native to bathrooms. What appears to be fine cabinetry is actually a series of ready-made kitchen-cabinet doors. Shower curtains are linen in the same unicorn print as the wallpaper (a plastic liner protects the fabric). Blue-and-white scheme is repeated in the fixtures and in the tiles which combine two contrasting shapes—curved for the floor and square cut for the counter top and walls behind the tub.

A romantic, luxurious mood, *right,* is evoked by the lavish use of onyx in a bathroom, plus the provocative interplay of contemporary design, a kind of Roman splendor, and a touch of turn-of-the-century whimsy. The transparent stool base and curved, metal plant stand, efficiently designed lavatory with a long reach of mirror over it and excellent lighting recessed behind textured glass in the ceiling, are all beautifully complemented by a window of Tiffany glass that is never concealed. A telephone-type shower fixture eliminates the need for a shower curtain. Reigning supreme is the superb onyx. Architect: Arthur L. Finn.

TALENTED ROOMS
BATHROOMS

1 One mirrored wall doubles the width of a narrow bathroom—and also doubles the pretty impact of an antique flowered rug, a collection of old prints, and a Victorian towel rack sprayed gold. The ledge behind the tub is just wide enough to hold a few dainty bibelots. Interior design: Michael Taylor.

2 Permanently bright sunshine in the form of planks of yellow Formica enlivens a small bath in guest quarters of a weekend house. Open shelves provide a nice, help-yourself way to store towels. Interior design: David Barrett.

3 Big panels of clear glass bound in brass protect a fabric-covered wall around a tub. Favorite pictures, simply framed, are high enough to be safe from splashes.

4 One charming paisley pattern over all—wall tiles, fixtures and ceramic fittings—dresses up what would have been a bland, minimal bathroom in a remodeled farmhouse. Interior design: Peter Prince.

5 Flowered borders of bright morning glory tiles spread delight around the tub and planter in a garden-bathroom. On the wall by the shower, a series of butterfly tiles calls attention to the soap shell. Interior design: Rodolfo Ayala.

6 An unexpected treasure house in a guest bath is an antique dresser lacquered red and decked out with a copper lavatory, old brass fittings, a mirror and, for more surprise, a collection of old plates. Interior design: Charles Dear.

7 Vertical strips of frosted bulbs flank the mirror in a man's bath, creating excellent light to shave by. The yellow counter and dark-stained cedar walls echo colors of the adjoining dressing room.

8 Tubside comforts—an upholstered chair, good lamp, table for magazines, soft carpeting and a painting on the wall—turn a bathroom into an updated version of the withdrawing room. Interior design: R. & R. Robinson, Inc.

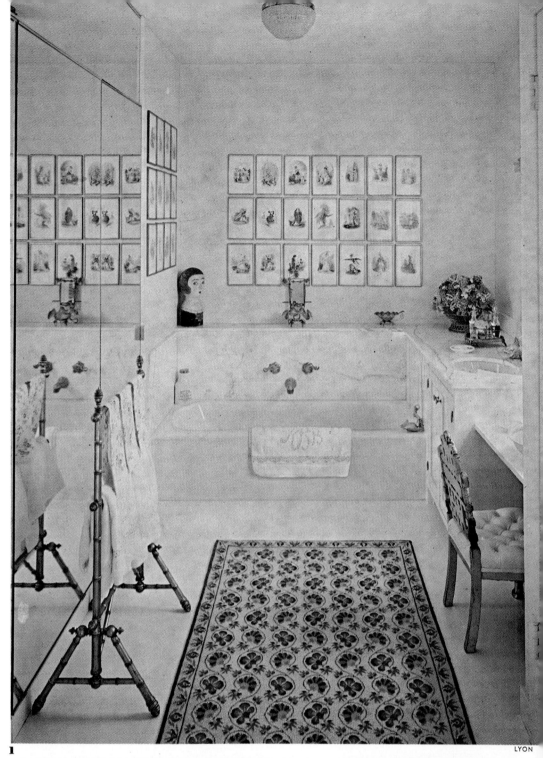

1   LYON

2   MAYA

3   GAIN

4

5

6

7

8

Small pond of a tub, *left,* is specially shaped for luxurious toe-stretching and equipped with a therapeutic whirlpool device. The TV set on one wall has remote controls beside the sunken tub. Nearby is a couch for after-bath napping and a table for conveniences. Opposite, sliding doors lead to a walled terrace for sunbathing.

Delightful oasis, *above,* a free-standing tub enclosed in mosaic tile and ringed with a marble ledge, conveys the message that this is truly a room for unhurried bathing. Between the silk curtains are small fold-back screens paneled with fabric to match the wall covering. When pulled across, they ensure privacy without cutting off daylight streaming through the upper parts of the glass. Interior design: James Leslie, Jr.

Redwood sauna, *right,* an increasingly popular auxiliary of the American bathroom, conveniently adjoins the master bedroom of a Florida house. Inside the doorway are a heater and receptacle for rocks on which water is dashed to produce a salubrious atmosphere. The upper shelf is for reclining in higher, hotter air. Interior design: Darrell Fleeger.

Independent island, *far right,* in a bathroom, has two basins recessed in the 5-foot-diameter marble top. Separating them: a ceiling-high, three-sided mirror that gives fascinatingly complex reflections of the room and terrace. Architect: Harold W. Levitt.

TALENTED ROOMS
BATHROOMS

223

ECKERT

ASHLEY

BRIGHT

Topiary trees, *above,* topped by rakish birds, adorn a guest bath. The tile designs are all it takes to enliven the simple room. Interior design: Ernestine Cannon.

Three tiers of cabinets, *left,* provide much storage and charm in a high-ceilinged bath carefully remodeled to restore its original Victorian aura. Behind the wood-paneled doors are the less decorative necessities; gleaming through glass fronts is a collection of barbers' antique bottles. Stained glass windows, augmented by shutters, afford intriguing light while preserving privacy. Interior design: Wallace Kay Huntington.

Bathroom-study, *left, below,* is a pleasant reality, thanks to astute planning that turned an extra bedroom into a man's spacious retreat. Along one end wall: a blue-tiled tub, flanked by a shower and toilet behind louvered doors. (On the opposite wall is the lavatory.) The antique table is handy for after-bath working, reading the paper, enjoying a cup of coffee. Architect: Wiard Ihnen.

Spirited design, *below,* of an intense blue-and-white wallpaper, zips up white tiles and fixtures. The antler motif is repeated by real pairs used as towel racks.

GRIGSBY

Sweeps of slate, *above,* pave a baronial bath in a remodeled barn. A spiral staircase leads to the master bedroom; an armoire holds clothes as well as linens. Tilting two-way mirrors allow the man of the house to shave comfortably while standing in the sunken tub, and also serve the double-basin lavatory counter, *far right.* The slate-topped chest, *right,* stores medicines. Interior design: Richard Heimann.

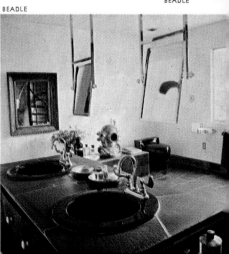

CHILDREN'S ROOMS

SMALL WORLDS THAT SPELL "SECURITY"

A child's domain must surely be the most versatile and delightful of rooms. It is play place, museum and warehouse for the youngster's myriad belongings, bedroom, study—and private retreat. Since it is his alone, the furnishings must be to his liking, with nothing pretentious and nothing difficult to care for. Let the vivid colors children love pinch-hit for fussy effects, and keep brightness and pattern to easily switchable curtains, washable rugs, spreads. Like an excellent story-book with a sprinkling of well-chosen, grown-up words, a child's room will be all the better if you include a few good pieces to whet his appetite for fine design. If you choose these with an eye for the different uses they may be put to in later years, your investment will be extra worthwhile. Do see, too, that the room has first-rate storage and lighting, and areas where cherished projects will be inviolable. For sizable activities, separate playrooms—where din can have a field day—are ideal.

Now and future furniture, *below,* are one and the same in a girl's room designed to grow up with her. A long bed is cozy in a niche; a rattan chest is superb as a catchall for any age; the chair holds two children or one adult. Coloring-book gaiety comes largely from furnishings that are easily changed to suit new tastes.

High and low delights, *right,* of color and pattern, make a little girl's room a bright playground. The garden fabric even wraps the bed's soaring posts and a big toy chest. For table work, flower-like stools; for floor play, carpeting in a green that grounds the multicolor scheme. Interior design: John FitzGibbons.

GRIGSBY

YEE

BAKER

GRIGSBY

**TALENTED ROOMS
CHILDREN'S
ROOMS**

Camelot canopies, *above,* of felt,
create a touch of make-believe
in a youngster's busy, multi-purpose
room. They also soften the lines
of the tall shelves and space-dividing
desk. The white-walled enclave is
further warmed by more red in
the painted floor and bulletin board,
and by the open storage of favorite
possessions. Interior design: Mac II.

High-rise shelves, *left,* accessible
from both sides, subtly divide the
territory of a room-for-two
without sacrificing play space.
Each child also has an equal share of
the clean-lined furniture, chosen
for its long-range capabilities.
Unmatched spreads and the freshness of
polka dots, large and small, add to
the fun. Interior design: Emily Malino.

Cheer by the yard, *far left,* makes
the most of simple furnishings
in a little girl's domain. For
contrast, a plaid shade, and
mirror-backed shelves on white
walls. Interior design: Blaine & Booth.

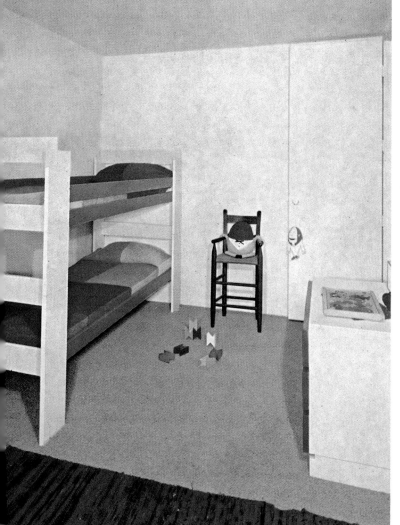

GRIGSBY   LEONARD   LEONARD

Expanses of white, *above,* on unadorned walls and tall doors, promote a feeling of added space and make it possible to use bunk beds without having a small room look cramped. White is also a wonderful background for the bright colors children love. Bed rails and drawer fronts of the chest are painted to go with plaid blankets that double as bedspreads. Interior design: Edward Diehl of Design Research.

A trundle bed, *above, right,* pulls out to accommodate a young guest in close quarters. A desk-counter under the window turns a tiny pocket of space to good use. Next to it, a long closet neatly hides odds and ends as well as clothing. Interior design: Edward Diehl of Design Research.

Vivid colors, *right,* give a room warmth despite a total absence of rugs, curtains, frills. Designed for two pre-teen girls, the bedroom's largest outpouring of orange is in cotton contour spreads with mattress platforms covered to match. Minor splashes come from a high chair bequeathed to a favorite doll, many books and the printed fabric window shades. A second, plain pair of shades veils the upper shelves. Interior design: Emily Malino.

GRIGSBY

GRIGSBY

Sweet-sharp sophistication, *left,* of lemon, young green and white, brings on a bright mood in a teen-age daughter's room. The chintz's pattern and the furniture's stinging color are balanced by equal emphasis.

Rugged materials, *left, below,* are clearly called for in a growing, active boy's room. Plasticized hardboard walls never need painting, have a pleasant marbleized pattern. Vivid blankets are spreads, too. Bench and toy cart on casters roll under the bunk beds. Interior design: Bill Lanyon.

Dramatic designs, *right, top,* and smashing colors have the verve a teen-age girl likes—and they are made of practical stuff, besides. A Moorish canopy bed is wicker, given a new dash with magenta paint. The quilted spread in polished cotton is the same rich hue. Sunflowers printed on the wallpaper and curtains are more vivid than real. For contrast: a pale pink throw rug and table skirt. Floor, patterned like river gravel, is light, breeze-to-clean vinyl.

A quest for privacy, *far right, top,* plus a teen-age girl's hankering for a romantically feminine atmosphere, are nicely satisfied by a room with the versatility of an apartment. One print is used lavishly and even frames the sofa-like bed delightfully with curtains. A coffee table and pull-up wicker chair help make the retreat look less like a bedroom and more like a sitting room. Interior design: Layne-Reale Assoc. Inc.

Garden haven, *right,* for a young daughter, has the natural seclusion and green vistas that come from fringing woods. The fabric, deep pink on white, and a rug, the palest of violets, add soft flower colors. Hung in lieu of curtains are slim folding panels with matching fabric insets. Interior design: Robert Wedel.

STOLLER

LEONARD

MCKEVITT

INDOOR PLAYGROUNDS

A playroom is apt to be the liveliest place in the house. And the noisiest. A setting as isolated and impervious to sound as possible and furnishings that are models of fortitude will give youngsters freedom to have fun—and parents freedom from nagging. Keep in mind the room is mostly a daytime one. Try to incorporate much daylight, outdoor views, access to a stretch of lawn. Happily, many rugged building and decorative materials are colorful and gay, so you can easily create a cheerful mood. To make the most of space, consider built-ins and adaptable, stackable furniture. Then, at night, the room will be able to take on new roles for adult parties.

VAN GAALEN

VAN GAALEN

Racket room, *above and right,* was especially designed to take the hectic meetings of cub scouts. The basement gathering place is almost boy-proof, with its random width paneling, acoustical ceiling tiles, leisure carpeting and rugged stools. Movable tables, one for stand-up work, one of sit-down height, are plastic-topped. Each has built-in containers for tools. For family relaxation: a fireplace recessed in an existing chimney, and a cushioned window seat.

Quick-change gym, *far right,* between children's rooms and dining area of a one-story house, is stamping ground, by day, for three sons. Treetop views plus solid colors repeated several ways enliven the huge room. For adult parties, apparatus is cleared and replaced by candle-lit tables for eight. Later, tables are removed and the floor is given over to dancing. Architect: Stanley Salzman of Edelman & Salzman.

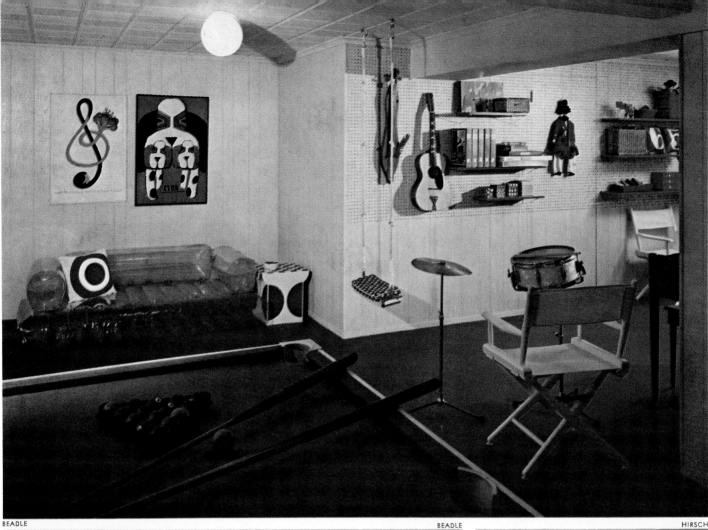

Two-story fun room, *left,* with its madcap color scheme, has an exhilarating sense of play. In the children's wing of a vacation house, the spacious room connects with a large deck and two floors of bedrooms. The play area resembles an art show of giant canvases abounding with wallops of color. A junior gym, it has space for running around on rainy days, a marvelous altitude for rope-climbing, areas for table games, too. Even clean-up can be fun, since the youngsters themselves can hose down the floor. Opposite the staircase is a wall of storage closets. Architects: Vernon and Jay Sears. Interior design: Brett Winston, Helen Wallace.

Music-and-game room, *above,* for a family's three teen-agers, takes over a formerly dreary basement, turning it into a lively place where they and their friends are free to make as much noise as they please. Acoustical tiles finish the ceiling, while vinyl tiles are on the floor. White paneling masks cinder block walls, water pipes and a heater-and-storage section. Free-standing stairway, *bottom, left,* was boxed in to create three closets (accessible from the other side), then papered. A pool table is used for Ping-Pong, *bottom, right,* when topped with two painted plywood panels. Along one wall, cupboards create a window seat niche.

TALENTED ROOMS
INDOOR PLAYGROUNDS

STUDIOS
AND
WORKROOMS

RETREATS
FOR CREATING
AND CONCENTRATING
AT HOME

Everyone needs a private enclave that caters to his particular interests or demands. In almost all houses there is some overlooked, suitable nugget of space waiting to be discovered and transformed into a studio, hobby area, workshop or office. A full-time, free-lance illustrator might need an entire room for his work; a sociable needlewoman, just a roomy basket by the sofa. Most work-at-home areas fall somewhere between: an available patch of floor and wall, easily taken from some room that will not miss it—then properly lighted and artfully fitted with adequate work surfaces, bins, file drawers and other conveniences for keeping paraphernalia in its place. A home office—for business or household paper work—can sometimes fit so neatly into the scheme of things that you scarcely notice the addition. A sewing corner, photographer's haunt or hobby center can often be tucked away in a closet or cabinet and concealed behind doors between sessions. The wherewithal of artists and craftsmen—bright yarns, jars of glaze, even woodworking tools—can make a delightful show of its own as well as give guests a glimpse of something special going on. Beginning here, a cache of talented work-at-home rooms, some wholly devoted to creativity, others with efficiently plotted private projects tucked into their pockets.

Tabletop atelier, *left*, puts an enamelist's bedroom to work to serve her craft. Specially designed table—a rectangle sprouting a curve—
holds glazes and kiln conveniently, occupies a sliver of well-lighted space.

Garden-house studio, *below*, lets an architect and his decorator wife pursue their careers at home without disrupting family routine.
Furnished with twin drawing boards and shelves, the one-room house
has its own terrace, ideal for consulting with clients when the weather is fine.

KERTESZ

237

1 Sunny family room contributes a corner, *left*, to a loom, a yarn winder and a store of yarn already wound (stacked in vivid-colored plastic vegetable bins), belonging to a professional weaver who also happens to be the lady of the house.

Elsewhere in the room, *below*, furniture and equipment encourage other family doings: lunch or a game such as chess at the round table, writing at the desk, tending the glorious hanging greenery or the pot garden that flourishes by the corner window. On a pegboard panel against the wall are spindles, yarn samples, sketches of macramé hangings and rya rugs to come.

2 Hand-tailored alcove, generously lit by under-cabinet fluorescents, condenses sewing room storage and gear into a scant 7 by 2½ feet. Between sessions, machine swings into the base cabinet, ironing board onto a nearby closet door.

3 Roomy closet develops into a small but uncramped darkroom, with U-shaped counter for enlarger and trays, shelves for measurers and timer. Under-counter compartments hold paper, chemicals and a gadget bag.

4 A guest room wall makes a surprisingly good workshop; its pegboard panel and cabinet keep tools neatly within reach of the carpenter at his workbench. The trim new tools plus curious old ones make a fascinating display on the wall.

5 One wall in a bedroom supports a personal office, complete with drawers, shelves, and writing surface that might well double as a dressing table. Interior design: Eszter Haraszty.

2

GUERRERO
SZASZ

3   STOLLER

4

5   KERTESZ

LEONARD

LEONARD

TALENTED ROOMS
STUDIOS AND WORKROOMS

LEONARD

Family crafts room, *above,* uses brilliant patches of
color to identify a stool, a hanging panel and, across the
room, *left,* a supply cabinet for each member of the
family. The sky-lit room opens onto its own walled patio
where craftsmen can spread out their work under the sky:
the ceramist can set up her kiln, the sculptor his stand
and the furniture maker can saw or sand without a care.

Chameleon home office, *right,* meshes so smoothly
with its guest room surroundings that the room's true
identity depends strictly on your point of view. A file
cabinet is the bedside table; the desk, with the
typewriter traded for a mirror, becomes a dressing table.
Daylight filters through sliding shuttered screens,
artificial light through the louvers of a ceiling panel.

VAN NES

Attic transformation, *above,* of neglected space into a one-room abode is due, in large part, to the clever use of otherwise wasted space under the eaves. An entire wall of built-ins is the clue to this room's adaptability. Open shelves at the far end house a TV and music center. Caned doors in the center conceal a drop-down bed, *right.* Behind other doors, *far right,* are dressing table or desk facilities and shelves for miscellany. (More cupboards and drawers flank the left side of the bed.) During the day, comfortable chairs and a love seat (on roll-away casters) invite relaxation. Across the room, a long table with storage units behind it, *left,* stands ready for all kinds of pursuits and can be cleared for dining. The neutral scheme is spiked with yellow ceiling beams, chairs, striped shades.

ONE-ROOM LIVING

CANNY CONQUEST OF SPACE

Creating a one-room realm where you can relax, sleep, eat and entertain with grace and comfort can be a challenging and fascinating enterprise. Begin by recognizing the limitations, but don't overestimate them. Given enough space, you can divide it quite easily into separate areas for specific purposes. If your room is L-shaped, you can use the ell for dining, sleeping—anything that makes the most sense. But if your room is a smallish square or rectangle, face the fact that every square foot of floor and wall space must work full time to serve your needs, gratify your eye and fulfill your desire for calm, uncluttered expanses. Whatever your floor plan, begin by deciding where to put a bed or beds that can double for seating during the day or fold up into the wall. If a coffee table or chairs have to be moved at bedtime, make sure they are easy to shift. Arrange your lighting for both living room and in-bed convenience. Decide at the outset exactly how many guests, if any, you can invite for seated meals without putting a crimp in before-and-after dinner circulation. Remember that buffet meals can be great fun and only require tiny tray-tables or other handy surfaces—even laps.

Neatness is essential to living attractively in one room, but regardless of how tidy you may be, it is impossible to cope unless you have adequate storage space—easily accessible for things you need often, and less so for other possessions. Besides making the most of the closets you have, consider cupboards and chests that go down to the floor, built-in storage walls or sections, large shallow boxes to put under sofa beds behind concealing skirts. Although organization is essential to living well in one room, so is your brand of highly personal, decorative appeal. This is the quality that gives a place significance, makes it uniquely your own—and home.

BEADLE

BEADLE

BEADLE

BEADLE

TALENTED ROOMS
ONE-ROOM LIVING

Blithe gaiety, *left,* permeates an artist's domain that consists of one light-filled room in which she works and lives. The basic ingredients: white walls, window shutters and shaggy area rug; light floorboards, cane and wicker; vermilion for vitality; an old porter's chair for fun. Painting materials are stowed away in baskets on simple metal shelf units when not in use. A minimum of furniture gives a sense of space, but pillows scattered on the floor make big parties possible at any time.

Dramatic impact, *above,* of deep blue walls, scarlet sofas, reaches of pure white, and transparent tables, is strengthened by the bold way each color is massed. A sizable, nonworking fireplace, *top right,* now used as a bar, divides the long, narrow room into two areas—one end for lounging on the red sofas, the other end for dining, studying or writing in front of a fall of white curtains. Stretching along the opposite wall is a long banquette, *right,* backed with pillows, all white from end to end. At night it makes up into two comfortable beds, *below.* For further drama: a pair of molded, white side chairs and a low cylinder of diffused, soft light.

Chapter 7

PROFESSIONAL EXPERTISE

The trained talent
that
can translate
your ideas
into personal realities

HOW TO WORK WITH AN ARCHITECT

Unless your motives for wanting an architect-designed house are well defined and meaningful to your family, you diminish your chances of getting a house that is genuinely gratifying to you *or* your architect. For it is a fact that most architects believe they do their best work for clients who know what they want and understand the complex process they are letting themselves in for.

So let us assume your motives are keen, and your needs, wishes and predilections are sharply focused. How do you go about finding *the* architect? Many do not accept residential design work. The most commonly expressed reason—the inability to make a modest profit or even to break even—is made more poignant by the widespread admission that all talented designers "should try," as one architect put it, "to fit houses into the cracks of their practice."

In every region, however, there are some excellent men who do accept residential commissions, and ungrudgingly. Don't look for them in the Yellow Pages. They will be listed there, but their capabilities won't be. In any case, having an architect-designed house is almost never the result of an impulse decision; nor should it be. The idea most often ferments slowly over months and even years. Typically, your awareness is sharpened and your interest quickened by the houses of friends, the houses you see in magazines, the houses that catch your eye while driving past them.

Once you have decided that now is the time, a thorough canvas of designers is advisable. If you find an architect in your community whose work appeals to you, well and good. But you needn't stop there. Fan out beyond your immediate locality if necessary. Be willing to seek out and evaluate the houses of architects whose offices may be located a hundred or so miles away. Distance is not likely to be a deterrent, providing all other circumstances are favorable.

A leading architect and a teacher of architects, William Wilson Wurster, has said, "Houses are built by husbands and wives in the happiest period of their lives, and architects, unlike lawyers and doctors, have to be thankful they are dealing with optimists." There is another peculiar reason why architects, although professional men like lawyers and doctors, differ from them. A lawyer's clients make no pretense of grasping the intricacies of the law; but an architect's clients come to him with a hatful of pragmatic ideas, convictions and prejudices

about his profession. "Everyone is an expert on houses," another architect notes, "because everyone lives in one."

Undeniably, the optimism Dean Wurster has observed in house-building husbands and wives has its uses. The stakes, both subjective and financial, are high, and the occasions for self-doubt can occur with the regularity of sheep jumping over stacks of two-by-fours. But more than optimism—in the beginning, at least—you will need a healthy sense of realism. If your architect is the conscientious man you wish him to be, he will hope to learn a great deal about you and your family. Some architects recommend that a family put their thoughts in writing before the first serious discussion, and some families respond with remarkably voluminous and evocative descriptions of themselves and their preferences.

It is axiomatic that a client wants more than he can afford. That's all right. Only by spreading out all of your ideas on the table (sometimes literally, in the form of magazine pages, ads, brochures and whatnot) can the two of you separate the must-haves from the wish-we-coulds. Keep in mind, however, that a house is not a jigsaw puzzle. The pieces do not always fit where you wish they would, which is why you hire an architect. His challenge is to achieve a balance of all elements, material and spatial. The balance can be tipped, of course, if your family's special interests and needs warrant it. For example, an airline pilot with a passion for electronic gadgets persuaded his architect that these should preempt an incredibly disproportionate part of the budget. "The house was little more than a container," says the architect, "but the client was happy." And so, presumably, was his family.

Starting with the Site

Nearly all of your decisions will be conditioned in one way or another by the size of your budget. For example, if you have not yet bought your site, this investment obviously can have a great bearing on the size and quality of the house itself. Land has never been scarcer or more costly than it is today. Given a choice, the architect would prefer that you do not have a site when you come to him. It is a legitimate part of his service, for one thing, to help you find one. For another, he should be familiar with both available land and a fair price for it. But his main concern—and the one for which you pay him—is one of design. To him, a site is roughly analogous with an artist's canvas; what he puts on it should be determined in large degree by the size, shape, contour, the immediate surroundings and any worthwhile view.

Tell the architect exactly how much money you wish to spend. But keep in mind that the bills do not stop coming in when the last workman quits the premises. In your very natural eagerness to have the best house and the best materials, you may be tempted to forget two elements which are essential in any successful home: landscaping and furnishings. Don't forget them. If you have to endure the next ten years apologizing (to yourselves, if no one else) for the crop of milkweed outdoors and the makeshift furnishing indoors, is the adventure worth the effort? You won't be happy with a shell of a house, and it is likely that the architect will share your discontent.

It is true that many houses exceed an agreed-upon budget, but the blame is difficult to assess. Typically, the culprit is good intentions, shared by client and architect. "We've just got to have that extra bathroom," you say. "Well, I'll try to squeeze it in," says the architect. And there goes the budget irretrievably.

One architect who has designed hundreds of houses and kept them within the budget tells his clients point-blank that three variables determine the substance of a house: the size of the budget, the amount of space and the quality of materials and equipment. Any two of these three variables may be made definite stipulations. But the third must be left flexible, with the architect permitted to reach decisions that will keep the whole project in balance. Thus, if you were to agree on a hard-and-fast budget and insist on a full voice in choosing what goes into the house, then you would be expected to rely on this architect's judgment where space is concerned. Such an understanding can contribute to a fruitful working relationship, since any layman can readily grasp the physical essentials of a house when spelled out in these terms.

Architects feel strongly that you should be able to have the things you most want in your house. These can be almost anything—from compartmented baths for the children, to walnut paneling in the study, to a greenhouse. Or your wishes may involve planning considerations: clear-cut zoning between the areas for adults and children, a garage facing away from the street or a conveniently placed darkroom near the master bedroom.

These and dozens of other personal wants should be thoroughly aired before the architect begins his preliminary sketches. For once he has moved from the conference phase of planning to the drawing board, it is his professional prerogative to do what he is best at, designing, without major additions or amendments to your program.

Preliminary sketches usually will be drawn for your consideration in a matter of several weeks. The sketches can serve two important purposes. They will give you a comprehensive view of the proposed floor plan, the various elevations and the siting of the house. In addition, the architect may ask one or more contractors to give him a cost estimate. If the contractor has worked with the architect before and is confident that his final working drawings will not depart widely from the preliminary sketches, the estimated cost can effectually allay your budget anxieties.

Finished *working drawings* are what the layman calls blueprints. They are the plans on which contractors' bids are based. Copies are supplied to all subcontractors (for carpentry, plumbing, heating, electrical work, etc.), and their workmen follow them throughout the entire construction. *Specifications* for the house are drawn up by your architect, and they constitute an agreement between you and the contractors. They describe in detail the types of materials and equipment to be used, the manner in which they are to be installed, and even how the workmen are to clean up after the work is finished. Specifications are a safeguard.

In the Architect's Hands

Having spent weeks and even months cultivating a lovely relationship with your architect, you have now reached the time, as construction commences, when he alone calls the turn. Few exasperations can compare with those of the architect and builder when confronted with a client family that camps on the job, offering gratuitous advice and requesting last-gap changes in the blueprints. No one supposes that you should meekly suppress your thoughts when you *see* slipshod work or structural mistakes being committed. But it is your architect's responsibility to represent your interests at the construction site. His fee, as recommended by the American Institute of Architects, a reliable source, is 15 per cent of the construction costs up to $250,000.

As the house nears completion, many families begin to think about retaining two other professionals (if they can afford them) —a landscape architect and an interior designer. But this is too late for best results. Ideally, the landscape architect should be on the scene when a site is being chosen; and if not then, certainly when the house is being sited and future planting is under consideration. Those first steps can be decisive.

An interior designer's skills are best introduced at early conferences, when personalities, tastes and family makeup are being taken into account. Also, because there may be conflicts between the architect and interior designer, it is wise to bring them together at the start. The interior designer's principal role is to select the furniture, furnishings, colors, fabrics, accessories.

If you plan to use the services of a kitchen planner, he, too, should arrive on the scene early. His concerns are literally measurable. How large should the kitchen be? How much building budget is to be spent on equipment that goes into this most expensive and pivotal room? The kitchen planner, the architect and you need to answer these questions to your mutual satisfaction before the architect draws his first line.

Is having an architect-designed house worth all the trouble? No, if you are a bargain hunter. Contrary to the arguments of wishful thinkers, an architect in most instances cannot be expected to save you money, and the good ones make no such claim. But he can, in many cases, design and help you build a better house, a house more responsive to your family's requirements, than any you might happen onto in your local housing market.

Some families hire an architect for prestige. They want a "name" designer and too often get a house embodying most of *his* values, few of their own. Yet such an imbalance in favor of the architect is not always a thing to be deplored; some people feel their lives can be enriched by living with "architecture." But they are not typical.

The happiest of all motives for wanting a house uniquely yours grows out of a zest for expanding your horizons and enlarging your experience. It has a great deal to do with a family's optimism, but also with its imagination and sense of purpose. In a letter to a young designer, Frank Lloyd Wright wrote: "Building can be fun, but it should assume a serious obligation." He might well have expressed the same sentiment to any young couple who asked him to design a house for them, and you may well take his advice.

HOW TO WORK WITH AN INTERIOR DECORATOR

Anyone can furnish a room; there's no trick to that. To *decorate* a room is something else again, and the difference is not one of aesthetics alone. Comfort, suitability, individuality must all be inherent in a room to make it really satisfying. To integrate shapes and materials, colors and patterns, light and shadow, in such a manner that they create a livable and personable environment for the client is the decorator's goal. But he can reach it only if you know how to work with him in the right way. That way begins long before you actually sit down to discuss your wants. First, you need a knowledge of what these professionals can do for you, how they differ, and what they cost. The next step is to find the decorator who can best interpret your wishes at your price, because you cannot work the right way with the wrong person.

What a Decorator Can Do

A trained decorator (and no others are worth discussing) is more accurately an interior designer—a definitive title you should be aware of, whether you use it or not. Many house painters, furniture salesmen and managers of slipcover workrooms call themselves "decorators." But interior designers are professional men and women, qualified by education and experience to create interiors, and they have named their two national organizations accordingly: the long-established American Institute of Interior Designers (A.I.D.), and the National Society of Interior Designers (N.S.I.D.). Both have exacting membership requirements, so either set of initials after a deco-

rator's name already gives you some clue to his competence, although many non-members are highly proficient, too.

An interior designer can assemble and put together all or part of the furnishings of any room and interpret all periods of design, although he (or she) may personally prefer one to another and be better known for his favorite. He can begin with empty space or make the most of your favorite possessions by giving them a new setting, redesigning furniture that warrants it, having other pieces refinished or reupholstered. He can design furnishings to meet specific situations or create special effects. And his designing ability is not limited to furnishings alone. A professional interior decorator is competent to design closets, bookcases, lighting and other installations.

An interior decorator can save you endless footwork, because he knows exactly where to find anything you want. Furthermore, his field of choice is much broader than yours, because some of the most dis-

tinguished furnishings are available only through decorators. A decorator also knows the reliable workrooms, some of which cater exclusively to the decorating trade. You can rarely, on your own, get the same quality of labor and service that is available to professionals or expect the same loyalty.

Finally, a reliable decorator makes himself responsible for everything connected with your job. Such assurance is worth a good deal—for peace of mind alone.

What a Decorator Cannot Do

A decorator cannot, however, read your mind. As a result of experience and observation, he may deduce that you prefer cool elegance to informal charm, or Georgian to Louis XV, but that would be only an educated guess. He cannot be sure of the way you and your family like to live, and he most definitely needs to be clued in on personal idiosyncrasies, such as a dislike for all Oriental design.

An interior designer cannot see your bank account and decide how much you can afford to spend. He cannot foresee the possible snags that may come up in connection with the job. He may take the greatest precautions, but events and incompetence beyond his control—delayed deliveries, discontinued items—can upset the most carefully calculated timing.

Before you start looking for a decorator, you should understand the distinction between an independent and one who is affiliated with a large department or furniture store. Each offers you certain conveniences. Thus, an independent interior designer may work on his own or be the head or a member of a decorating establishment. He or she goes to your house or apartment to size up exactly what you need and want and to supervise the job until its completion. He works out floor plans, assembles color schemes, obtains fabric samples. He takes or sends you to decorator showrooms, antique shops and other places, to look at furnishings he thinks will be suitable, or he helps you make selections from pictures in catalogs. He may also own a small decorative specialty shop.

Among the independent decorators, a one-man or one-woman operation is usually highly personal and often outstandingly good. But be very sure of your choice before you use a decorator who has no office at all and is not a member of the A.I.D. or N.S.I.D. In some communities, it is still all too easy for a rank amateur to assume the title, "interior decorator."

The decorating department of a very large store may be staffed with as many as thirty accredited interior designers, plus draftsmen, shoppers and other assistants. The decorators work exactly as they would in an independent decorating establishment and use outside-the-store resources at will. In addition, the decorating department in a big store offers certain services. First, a limited amount of free advice is available—the kind that can be given right in the store. Second, you can take advantage of any payment plans the store may have. Third, a store decorator can sell you any furnishings the store carries, many of which may be modestly priced and not available to independent decorators, because they are sold *only* through department and furniture stores.

What a Decorator Costs

The independent decorator makes his profit in one of three ways: the first and most customary way is to buy everything at a discount and charge you the retail prices. Two other billing procedures are based on the exact cost of everything to the decorator *plus* either a prearranged percentage of that cost or a flat fee for the entire job.

You also pay: a decorator's out-of-pocket expenses for travel and so on; any sales taxes, shipping, trucking and storage charges; the price of blueprints, renderings and models; the costs of any revisions or changes you may make in your order after it is placed; and fees for supervision beyond the amount the decorator deems reasonable for the successful completion of your job.

In spite of such standard practices, however, you may still discover that one interior designer will give you an estimate of, say, $5,000, and another name twice that price. The difference more often lies in the quality of the furnishings than the quality of the taste. A clever decorator can use such elements as color, scale and surprise to great effect; you pay for only the cost of average furnishings and the priceless ingredient of invention is thrown in for free.

In paying a decorator's bill, installments are usual. You pay a third at the beginning, after you have decided what you want and your decorator has drawn up an itemized estimate (not a contract, as many prices cannot be guaranteed at this time). You pay another third a little later, after the furnishings have been ordered but before delivery—and the balance on completion. But arrangements for payment differ, and the one way to be sure is to ask.

Many independent decorators and store decorating services give professional advice for a fee based on the time involved. It is money well spent if you want to ascertain an interior designer's customary price bracket and get a knowledgeable opinion about probable expenses. Should you subsequently decide to give the consultant your job, the fee for the first discussion will be credited to your account.

How to Choose a Decorator

To avoid wasting time, do your homework concerning costs before you start thinking about any specific interior designer. You may find that your field of choice is, of necessity, limited. It would be pointless to discuss the details of a $2,000 job, for example, with someone who thinks in terms of $10,000 minimum.

If you can, track down possible candidates through their work. You may see examples you like in the houses of friends, furnished model apartments or houses in new building projects, design centers in large cities, settings in stores, pictures in magazines. Or you can go to the decorating department of a dependable store and make an appointment. However you proceed, be sure to see pictures or actual examples of the decorator's work before you make the final decision to choose him or try elsewhere.

If yours is a very special project such as a one-room apartment to be done on a shoestring, try to find a decorator who specializes in that because it may not be everyone's forte. If he turns down the job, be grateful for his honesty and ask him to suggest someone else. And remember that the decorating departments in large stores can usually handle any job at a price within reason.

Working with a Decorator

If you are building a house or remodeling, bring your decorator into the planning as early as possible so he can work right along with the architect or builder. Decisions such as the designs of built-in storage, the location of electric outlets, the material or finish of floors, should be made during the construction stage; they become more costly later.

The first conference generally takes place in the decorator's office. Begin by telling him how much you intend to spend and what you hope to get for that sum. He may disenchant you right away or suggest various compromises, but he cannot proceed at all without an honest statement first from you.

Once the two of you have worked out the broad approach and defined the limitations, your decorator will want to know a lot more—the kind of life you live, the size of your family, the amount and nature of your entertaining. An experienced decorator will ask you many leading questions and is entitled to thoughtful answers. He will want to know about your tastes: what you like and dislike. Immediate elimination of the latter will save time. Above all, describe the mood you want—quiet or dramatic, old-world or new-minted, sophisticated or informal.

Be careful not to impose on the decorator's time. Indirectly, you are paying for it; the more minutes you waste, the less he can give to service and selection. Do not pester him with unnecessary telephone calls and stick to the subject when you talk to him.

Try not to vacillate. Make firm decisions, and do not change your mind unless you are prepared to pay for it. A skilled decorator will not allow you to make mistakes *provided you listen to him.*

It goes without saying that there is no point in working with an interior designer unless you have confidence in him. You don't need to be knowledgeable about decorating; that is his profession. But you should be honest with him about yourself and what you want. You should also make yourself responsible for the small touches that will put your signature on your room or house. Every interior designer worth his salt wants to express his client's personality, which means that he needs you as much as you need him. Together, you can work wonders.

How well does the average kitchen planner fill his multi-faceted role? If your knowledge is based solely on your friends' experiences, you may have a number of contradictory impressions.

One woman, whom you know to be exacting, is so pleased with her new kitchen that she becomes an instant demonstrator at the slightest flicker of interest on the part of any visitor. "It is exactly what I've always wanted," she says, "only better."

Another friend tells you, "I can't stand even thinking about what we went through." Her husband, still smarting from the experience, leaves the room, and she spends the next half hour telling you about it. Summation: they spent a small fortune and never did get the one item she wanted—a rotisserie in the oven. "Imagine! The planner returned $23 and said, sorry, he couldn't get the right part—something about the model I chose not being available."

If you are remodeling your present kitchen or installing a new one in another part of the house, the problems are apt to be complex, since considerable ripping out is likely to be involved (old appliances, tiled surfaces, even walls), and the existing arrangement of plumbing and heating lines may have to be changed. For such jobs, professional expertise is vital.

Even if you are merely planning to update your present kitchen on a piecemeal basis, the wise course would be to search out a qualified planner who is willing to prepare a long-range master plan. He can tell you which improvements would be the best investments to start with and which you can postpone.

The all-inclusive kitchen planner specifies the location of plumbing, gas and electricity inlets; plans the lighting; helps you plan the colors, fabrics and other decorative details; orders all materials (countertops, floor covering, wall covering, etc.); orders the appliances and cabinets; supervises all construction and installation; sees that all equipment performs as it should (initially; he can't be responsible forever).

Ideally, he is a single source of responsibility from beginning to end. He knows what materials and equipment are available and what is on the horizon. He is technically competent, aware of applicable building codes and knows the proper order of each step in the job. He is used to working with a plumber, electrician, mason, carpenter, painter and other specialists—which is highly important because, during installations, many different workers and their helpers are in and out and, when they are in, they are confined to working in a relatively small space that may hamper their efficiency.

"When you're remodeling a kitchen, you're dealing with—and disrupting—the nerve center of the house," observes a woman kitchen planner. "The well-qualified planner makes it as painless as possible."

Kitchen Planner at Work

In some big cities or big-city suburbs, you will find a few (a very few) independent kitchen planners who operate in much the same way as the independent decorator. Having no affiliations with manufacturers of appliances, cabinets or materials, such planners maintain no showroom and are free to recommend any make of equipment. Like the independent decorator, an independent kitchen planner works from an office (hopefully well stocked with catalogs and samples), accompanies his clients to

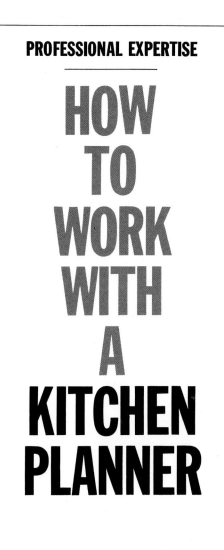

PROFESSIONAL EXPERTISE

HOW TO WORK WITH A KITCHEN PLANNER

manufacturers' showrooms and subcontracts the construction and installation to crews he works with regularly. Planners of this type are admittedly hard to find, but their number is growing rapidly.

Far more numerous are the kitchen-planning divisions maintained by authorized dealers for specific makes of cabinets or appliances. Often they, too, offer all-inclusive service (including decorating), but your choice of cabinets or appliances is limited to those of the manufacturer they represent. (If it is a cabinet manufacturer, you generally also have a choice of appliances and vice versa.) Some utility companies that sell appliances offer comparable all-inclusive planning services. Some firms that install only the cabinets they make to order in their own workshops also serve as dealers for one or two appliance manufacturers and provide a skeleton decorating service.

To help clear up the confusion over who is a qualified kitchen planner, a number of kitchen-planning firms of the dealer type belong to the American Institute of Kitchen Dealers. Among their membership requirements: evidence of financial stability; at least two years in the retail kitchen business; a showroom with at least one complete kitchen display that passes muster; and competent personnel.

If the kitchen is to be closely related visually to other rooms in the house—the family room, for instance—the kitchen planner should also be prepared to work closely with the decorator (or you, if you are your own decorator) over such matters as color schemes, curtains, the style of cabinets, the type of flooring.

The most common payment procedure is for the dealer or independent planner to submit an estimate for the completed kitchen, just as a contractor submits an estimate for a house. Prices for components and work of equal quality usually do not vary much within a given area. In any case, a difference of a few hundred dollars on a $4,000 job should not be crucial in anyone's decision. But if two estimates are as much as $400 or $500 apart, it would be well to treat the disparity as a warning signal. Does it mean a difference in quality, a misunderstanding on exactly what the job includes or something else? If both estimates are way beyond what you had expected, there may be other explanations. As one member of an established kitchen-planning firm points out: "The client may find she's in a higher price range than she intended because the professional planner, like an architect or decorator, brings to her attention what she wants and must have but hadn't thought of."

Once the plan and the price for the kitchen are agreed on, payment is usually made in three installments: 30 per cent on signing the contract, 50 per cent during the early stages of installation and 20 per cent upon completion. If the job is being financed by a bank loan or by extending the mortgage (as it can be), other arrangements may be worked out to your advantage.

The more informed you are about kitchens in general and your own needs in particular, the more confidence you will have in your selection of—and, later, in your dealings with—a qualified firm or individual kitchen planner.

The usual basic approach consists, of course, in reading kitchen-planning booklets and clipping ideas from magazines. Along with this homework, you might seek some general guidance from the home economist of your public utility company or Department of Agriculture extension services. Make a point, also, of going to see the kitchens on house tours and in model houses and apartments. And decide in advance to visit several kitchen showrooms. Once you become aware of the amazing range of components, accessories and gadgets available, you are less likely to be carried away, as one couple was, by the cabinet fittings in the first showroom they happened upon. Inebriated by gadgetry, they decided then and there that the man in that showroom was the planner for them. Too late they found out that one clever display doesn't make a professional planner, nor do accessories make a kitchen. Design comes first, fittings should be considered last.

The best lead in your search for a conscientious planner is, of course, an enthusiastic recommendation from someone you know. It would be wise, however, to get several opinions. To find out about a company's reputation, its stability in the community and so forth, check such sources as the local Better Business Bureau and Chamber of Commerce.

As you narrow down the candidates, ask them to let you see jobs they have completed. A kitchen planner may show you colored slides of actual kitchens or give you names of clients to call. When looking at these kitchens, immune yourself to color or style biases by keeping firmly in mind that

another family's taste may be far different from yours. Try to visualize and judge only the imagination and workmanship that went into the project.

Before you settle on any one company, be sure to ask questions:

Has the firm completed any *big* jobs? Will you be restricted in your choice of appliances? Some companies install only the makes they sell; others recommend and install whatever you choose. One-stop shopping has its pros and cons; consider them well. If the company sells appliances, does it expect you to call servicemen when a problem arises, or will it take on the responsibility of calling—and needling—them for you. Be wise and pose the question.

Don't hesitate to ask questions about the construction of the cabinets. "We want to educate the client as we go along," says one practical planner, "so that she knows what to look for and how to evaluate different estimates that we may give her."

Preliminary Discussions

When you have finished your sleuthing, the kitchen planner you have decided on will have his turn. Expect him to ask questions like these: How many eat in the kitchen? Which meals? Do you like to cook? Have you domestic help? Regularly or just for parties? How do you like to entertain? Is the storage you have now enough for all your dishes, glasses, etc.? Even: Do you plan to have more children?

When the planner comes to measure the kitchen, he will probably want to see the living and dining areas, to get an idea of your decorating preferences.

Stand up for your likes. For instance, do not get talked into ordering cabinets for every wall in the kitchen, when you know you prefer open shelves for certain areas. But recognize, too, that part of the kitchen planner's job is to push a little if a client's ideas are not forward looking enough or to put on the brakes if they seem too far out. If you insist you want this or that, you will probably get it. But perhaps you could get something better.

When clients see the first sketches, they are apt to react in one of two ways: they rave enthusiastically or angrily. The enthusiasts usually overlook the fact that a talented draftsman can make almost any plan look good on paper. The ranters fail to realize that first sketches are often feelers. The planner expects to consult, to discuss and to revise the plan to some extent. So do not

decide at first glance that his translation of your ideas is all right or all wrong.

Study the plan to decide if it is workable for you. Analyze the steps you would take in that kitchen to bake a cake, say. Visualize yourself getting eggs from the refrigerator there, a bowl from the cupboard here and so forth. And think hard about the maintenance that particular kitchen will demand. What about those louvered doors? Will you mind dusting them?

Before signing any contract, be sure to find out exactly what it includes. If you are remodeling an old kitchen, does the price cover tearing out the old equipment? (That could cost more than the new installations.) And who will be responsible for carting away ripped-out tiles?

Above all, ask how long the job will take. A designer who plots his installation jobs on charts estimates, for a simple L-shaped kitchen, one stoveless night, four or five days of inconvenience, a total of a week to ten days for actual completion, and, for an extensively remodeled kitchen, about three and a half to four weeks. But unexpected delays *can* develop.

Since so much goes on all at once when a kitchen is being installed, it is always possible for the unexpected to turn up, or the expected not to. A tool is inadvertently dropped on a counter top, marring it. Or the door is an unmistakable shade off in color from the new dishwasher. Be patient. Replacements take time. And a reputable planner *will* try to get you the results you want.

When the end is in sight, take time out from exultation to learn the correct maintenance procedures for your new kitchen. Any planner can cite examples of poor practices that cause breakdowns in appliances, materials, whatever—and lead to unwarranted criticism of the planner. Ask him or her how to clean counter surfaces, etc. Arrange for a home economist on the staff of the appliance manufacturer or your local utility company to demonstrate your new appliances *after* they are installed.

The kitchen is almost certainly the most expensive room in your house. And its design and organization demands more thinking and time and patience on your part than any other room. But it is also likely to be the most used, the one most closely associated with family life. Because of its hidden satisfactions as well as its real ones, having a great kitchen should, in the long run, be worth the most expert advice you can get.

Chapter 8

HISTORIC INSPIRATION

The President's Address

THE WHITE HOUSE

From historic houses that evoke periods of classic design and the hospitable ways of the past, we can acquire inspiration for our own homes. Since its recent restoration, the big white house at 1600 Pennsylvania Avenue in Washington, D.C. has become a monument of extraordinary distinction—and a splendid source of decorating ideas. For almost 200 years, however, the White House has undergone exterior and interior metamorphoses that included the quixotic as well as the inspired. Thirty-one Presidents, as of 1970, and thirty First Ladies (President Buchanan was a bachelor) have lived in the mansion, each bringing possessions or acquisitions to enrich their temporary home. Their tastes were as varied as their budgets, and the look of the house changed for better or worse with each new president. John F. Kennedy's wife, Jacqueline, made it her goal and task to hunt down presidential memorabilia. With the Fine Arts Committee for the White House, she gave the rooms the historic authenticity and consistent elegance they now possess. Their primary appeal lies in the superb taste with which almost two centuries of traditional furniture, paintings and decorative treasures are assembled and used. Shown here are some of the highlights of this historic and ongoing American heritage, followed by rooms at Blair House where guests of the president stay during their state visits.

The Blue Room

The original furniture for this state room was imported from France by President Monroe, and has been restored to full glory or faithfully copied. The room is not simply on exhibit, however; it is a hardworking reception area, although more to look at than to sit in, as Mrs. Kennedy once put it. The room's architectural grandeur and formal character are fully played up by the elegant damask wall covering. Against one wall, a huge painting, restored pier table and gilt chair—all beautifully related to one another—together create a grouping suited to the room's size. The walls' blue and gold damask is restated in miniature by the chair fabric, the portrait by the Washington bust, and the white trim by the marble of the table, which stands exactly where Monroe placed it. The white dado and pale parquet floor light up the room and link it with the adjoining Red Room.

LEONARD

LEONARD

The Green Room

Designed in the classic Adams and Jefferson style of 1800, the Green Room, *above*, is a parlor of shimmering elegance. Among its treasures are a lady's Baltimore desk, a Chippendale mirror above it that belonged to George Washington, and Henry Inman's portrait of Angelica Van Buren hanging high on the wall over a superb sofa that was once owned by Daniel Webster. This room is saturated with one color only, which is played up by white and held down by dark wood tones. White upholstery in a number of pale patternings relates furniture of different styles. White window trim shows to advantage because curtains and valances are hung within the handsome frames. Paintings hung high suit the scale of the room and complement tall windows.

The Red Room

Superbly restored in the manner of an American Empire parlor, circa 1817–1834, the Red Room, *right*, is the most used of the president's reception rooms. Its silk wall covering was copied from a fabric of the period, but all the furniture is old. Here, again, one color was chosen for walls, curtains and upholstery. It even appears again in the magnificent rug. The mantelpiece, pure Empire in the Napoleonic tradition, is a focal point for a furniture grouping. Curtains falling straight from ornamental rods accentuate the soaring height of the ceiling, which is further dramatized by the huge painting over the mantel. A woven border edges the curtains and frames the wall covering with a rich, scroll design that is ideally suited for the period.

LEONARD

Yellow Oval Room

First designed as a private sitting room, the Oval Room was appropriated by Dolley Madison as a ladies' drawing room, and swathed in yellow damask. Today, after many metamorphoses, it is once again a private sitting room, with the yellow legend revived. The president's favorite place for greeting guests before a state dinner, the room has furniture arranged in several hospitable groups, yet all are sufficiently open to make circulation easy. The largest grouping, in front of the fireplace, frames a patterned area rug over the room-sized rug. Handsome tables back up sofas that are out in the room, helping them to define more cozy areas without looking forbidding from the rear. Note how several matching, black-shaded lamps subtly link separate parts of the room. And observe that a picture on an easel comes into instant focus; that two paintings related in subject only, become excellent companions when hung together.

LEONARD

LEONARD

The White House

The Treaty Room

The Treaty Room

Winning its name from the many pacts signed within its walls, the Treaty Room is used today as a waiting and meeting rendezvous. Its furnishings are either historical or evocative of history. The awesome chandelier was one of three that President Grant ordered; the great table knew Andrew Johnson's gavel. The heart-back chairs were used in the Family Dining Room in the late 19th century. Less formal are the unmatched chairs at each end of the table, the swivel one dating from President Hayes' administration. Walls hung in a velvety, flock paper are paneled by a border that frames paintings and documents. The idea for the design, worth simulating with today's decorative self-adhesives, was copied from the paper in the room where Lincoln died across from Ford's Theater.

LEONARD

The President's Dining Room

Once a bedroom in the president's apartments, the room took on its present role with the installation of a kitchen and pantry next door, and the timely gift of handsome American Federal furniture. The most illustrious piece, the mahogany sideboard, was Daniel Webster's. The room's greatest glory, its spectacular wallpaper, is hung above a dado—so furniture will not cover any of the scenes. The paper's blue sky is echoed by the blue silk of the imaginatively hung curtains.

LEONARD

The Lincoln Bedroom

In this room, the most venerated in the White House, Abraham Lincoln signed the Emancipation Proclamation. Once Lincoln's Cabinet Room, it is now a guest room for the great, crowned or laureled. Much of the furniture was bought by Mrs. Lincoln—including the famous bed, which the president thought far too expensive. To keep the room from being ponderous and dark, yellow washes the walls, while translucent curtains, with just a swag for a valance, admit light.

Blair House is the home-away-from-home that our nation makes available to its guests during state visits to Washington. Handsome but not pretentious, the president's guest house is really two buildings with a party wall. The original house was built in 1824, but was not occupied by the Blair family until 1836. A generation later, Francis Preston Blair built the adjoining house for his daughter who married a cousin of Robert E. Lee. The two houses have since been unified under the Blair name, and remodeled to provide warm hospitality for visiting leaders, according to our standards of grace and comfort and theirs. The remodeling was done by a committee of government figures and private citizens who knew the welcome of Blair House would symbolize the welcome of our whole nation. Committee members collected original furnishings from the houses plus others expressive of the American tradition, and saw that the guest house had every facility for helping its occupants to carry out their business, and afforded them a place to relax from a taxing round of ceremonies. Today, Blair House is a summing up of our creative heritage in the arts and techniques of living—from the grace of fine and rare furnishings to the comfort of air-conditioning.

The Nation's Guest House

BLAIR HOUSE

The Blair-Lee Drawing Room

For visiting diplomats who often entertain guests during their stay in Blair House, the double drawing room on the Lee side of the house makes hospitality easy. Against backgrounds of restrained elegance, most of the furnishings—camelback sofas, armchairs, consoles, gilt and lacquer mirrors—are matched in important pairs. The old hand-painted Chinese wallpaper, an impressive acquisition, has echoes in the valances' pagoda-like styling, glazed Oriental lamps, figures on the mantel.

The entrance hall, *left*, small but without clutter, expresses distinction with a few choice pieces. The carved console is one of the house's original furnishings. Suited to it in scale is the decorative mirror, hung high to allow for a full arrangement of fresh flowers, always a welcome note.

The Lee Dining Room

The original Lee dining room, *left*, bigger of two in the combined Blair House structure, epitomizes a specific of hospitality, which is good eating. Notable appointments: the blue and white porcelain—some from the original Blair collection—and the needlepoint chair seats that repeat the china pattern. Each seat was worked by a Cabinet wife or a member of the redecoration committee. On the table, gold-rimmed butter plates set off the blue-bordered dinner plates; antique pistol-handled silver complements contemporary Danish crystal. Note: An Oriental rug is handsome and practical in a dining room.

The Blair Library

The fireplace end of the great library, *below*, in the King's Suite on the second floor, is a center for high-level conferences and conversation when a chief of state is in residence as a guest of the president and the nation. The woodwork, marble mantel, bronze Argand lamps and Queen Anne chairs were originally in the house. The huge Savonnerie rug was made in France for this room. Walls are painted a rich red glazed with umber. Strokes of blue—sharp for chair seats and a pillow, subtle in a printed fabric, pale and restrained on the handsomely decorated ceiling—accent the red and white scheme with a cool color.

LEONARD

LEONARD

LEONARD

The Lincoln Bedroom

Three highlights give the Lincoln Bedroom, *far left* and *left*, special luster: the American Empire secretary, amply satisfying any desk work requirements; gently colored paisley wallpaper; original sleigh bed. To give the high-ceilinged room a more intimate quality, the wallpaper is stopped at a relatively low height by a border, and more of the border frames the window. Note that identical shades relate unmatched lamps. The Lincoln Bedroom, as every guest room in Blair House, includes among its appointments monogrammed linens, *top right*, for bed and bath, plus blue-embossed fine writing paper, *right*.

Blair House Guest Rooms

The second floor of Blair House is planned as much for the private comfort and convenience of guests as the main floor downstairs is for public hospitality. Each guest room is equipped to serve all personal and official needs of the aides and ministers who accompany and assist their chief on missions of state. The two most important single rooms, apart from those for heads of state, are known as the Lincoln Bedroom and the Prime Minister's Bedroom. Both are rich in ideas.

Prime Minister's Bedroom

Sleep for a busy minister is wooed in a 19th-century, American mahogany four-poster, covered and curtained with English chintz. The tailored canopy is trimmed with a printed border that complements the pattern of the spread. A marble-topped Queen Anne table by the bed is among the best pieces in the house. Here again: a completely equipped desk.

Blair House

Blair House

The King's Bedroom

The bedroom of a visiting chief of state, *below*, is a fine example of an important period in American design. Curly maple furniture, cottons, linens and warm touches of red make the room less formal than other principal bedrooms in the house. Against one wall, a small desk, private and personal, is at the heart of beautifully arranged historic treasures. Specially embroidered red stitching outlines the wing chair's beige damask pattern; red and white tassels trim the white-on-white crewel spread and red-lined canopy.

The Queen's Bedroom

English 18th-century mahogany furniture and extremely luxurious fabrics are as elegantly formal in the Queen's bedroom, *right*, as the King's maple is simple. A creamy damask covers the chairs and upholsters a comfortable chaise elsewhere in the room. Lavender silks and satins are gathered in tieback overcurtains and the festooned valance, and also form swags on the bed's tasseled canopy and the dust ruffle. The dainty flowered pattern of the contemporary needlepoint rug is subtly restated on the two Derby porcelain lamps by the bed.

LEONARD

STORAGE A SOLVABLE PROBLEM

Not only have American families grown in size, but the number of possessions each of us owns has also skyrocketed. A much-admired architect told us that he asks his clients how much storage space they want and then he doubles it. They thank him for it. Think of the typical middle American family: husband who skis, and mows his own lawn, and shows his own films; wife who gives big dinner parties, and likes overnight guests, and paints on Sundays; older son who has his own musical group that rehearses and tapes in his room; daughter who makes closets full of clothing, and is seriously collecting rocks; preschool child who builds villages out of blocks. Think of all the *things* they have to put away.

Even if you are not building, you can still add the storage facilities that make the difference between exasperation and pleasure as you cook or sew or clean or pursue hobbies. To begin with, you can take your already existing closets and cupboards and reorganize them for greater efficiency. Is your front hall closet the usual type? If so, the rod is crammed full, but the floor and shelf space is used inefficiently. Replan this closet and you can probably double its storage capacity. Go on from there and try to work out a conveniently located filing system for everything from shoes to silver. Put each item where it can be seen and reached easily. Fasten shallow bins or shelves on closet door backs.

You can also find dead areas—under the bathroom lavatory, over the bathtub, under the stairs—and turn them into storage places. Almost any room can take some wall-hung shelves that weren't there before. Practically every informal area—kitchen, child's room, family room—has a space for lumberyard wallboard on which you can hang tools or toys or miscellany. In large rooms, if you can spare one or two feet of length or width, you can construct a whole wall of storage —open or closed or a combination —that will improve your daily lives and add visual interest to the room. An open mind and a conviction that the problem can be solved are the beginnings of a solution. This chapter shows all kinds of storage.

Family office closet, *opposite*, occupies the space of a former clothes closet whose single door was replaced by double ones. Upper space and door backs are cork tile-lined for pinups. Shelves of ¾ inch pine and commercial steel filing drawers are all gaily painted. Consolidated here are reference books, household records, correspondence and bills, too often scattered all over the house.

A storage hall, *this page*, runs 36 feet from foyer to service hall in a well-planned new house. Doors are flush, and streamers of color make the functional area most attractive. One closet, lined with perforated hardboard, holds sports gear; another has shelves for family luggage.

BEADLE

Double-depth china storage, *left,* on the upper half of a new storage wall that surrounds a refrigerator, is both decorative and practical. Plates, cups and saucers on shallow shelves fitted with racks are easily accessible and charming to look at. These rack sections swing out to reveal deeper shelves for serving pieces.

Planned silver closet, *below,* is lined with non-tarnish Pacific silver cloth. Loops on the door hold flatwear in easy-to-handle ranks, while the shelves hold all the hollow ware.

MIEHLMAN

Red-lined compartments, *below,* including two under the window, are differently shaped for convenient storage. Across the window: open shelves for displaying several pieces of sculpture.

ECKERT

GUERRERO

Copper pots and pans, *above,* occupy a whole kitchen wall, paneled in peg board and painted to match the room. Utensil outlines drawn on the wall insure the return of everything to its proper place.

Place mat trays, *below,* inside a cabinet, slide in and out, making table setting and clearing a snap. Napkins are also neatly stored here.

WARD

Everything for dining, *right,* is stored right in the dining room behind doors that are completely mirrored on the outside. Lining the china and glass compartments is washable, nylon suede cloth to prevent chipping. The silver drawers and shelves are lined with tarnish-preventing Pacific cloth. Fluorescent tubes light the closet interiors.

GRIGSBY

MAYA

Mat and napkin rods, *above,* on the wall behind the kitchen door, hold all the smaller table linens, making them easy to store, easy to use and free from creases.

GRIGSBY

Bar closet, *above,* made in an antique armoire, holds wines, liqueurs, spirits and glasses. The wines fit into a honeycomb system below the working shelf; the other supplies stand on shallow shelves that line three sides.

GRIGSBY

Glassed-in china closets, *above,* whose doors slide open, total twelve feet wide and go to the floor on one kitchen wall. In full view, but well-protected: china, glass, serving pieces, candlesticks and other table accessories.

273

YEE

WARD

Eye-level shoe shelves, *above,* help to make
the most efficient use of a closet. Other
bright ideas: out-of-season storage boxes,
both above shoes and below hanging jackets.
Full-length section for coats, dresses, is at the left.

Three kinds of space, *above,* in a closet for little
sisters, organizes their belongings: rod space,
shelf space, drawer space. The drawers are plastic
ready-made bins of varying depths, light enough
for a child to handle and an encouragement to neatness.

Overhead storage, *below,* is made reachable
by a ladder with velvet-upholstered rungs—
pretty and safely non-slippery. Hooks on the
panel between closet sections hold
umbrellas, items very often mis-stored or mislaid.

Shoes and shirts, *below,* share the same depth of
space in a man's clever pigeon-holed closet, in
which everything is visible and reachable in an instant.
Under the shirt shelves is the family safe,
hidden from casual view behind the doors of the closet.

A man's wardrobe, *below,* from
overcoats to socks, is filed away
all in one place. Thoughtfully planned
compartments within a closet make
a separate chest of drawers unnecessary.

STOLLER

STOLLER

GRIGSBY

A woman's glittering closet, *above,*
including banks of plastic drawers, shelves
edged with delicate fringe and sliding mirrored
doors, turns a large bathroom into a charming
dressing room as well. The color scheme:
pink and white and shiny brass, mirror-multiplied.

Masculine dressing room, *above, top,* does
not shut away the rod-hung clothes, since
it is enclosed and in an air-conditioned house.
Drawer storage is part of an all-plastic cabinet,
with space for everything from studs to sweat shirts.

Feminine dressing room, *above,* in the same
air-conditioned house as its masculine
counterpart, also stores a wardrobe uncloseted.
Nevertheless, garment bags in fabric to match the
wall pattern hold out-of-season and formal clothes.

STOLLER

Hard-working hall closet, *above,* not only takes care of coats but also contains shelves for games, compartments for folding chairs and tables and, since it has an outside wall, a shelf under the mail slot.

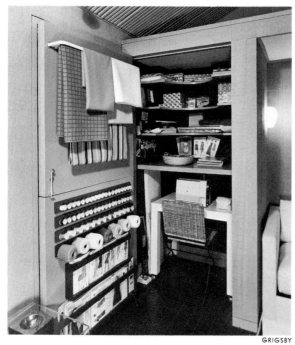

GRIGSBY

Sewing supplies, *above,* find a home in a carefully planned closet that has shelves for many essentials, a rod on the door for fabric, and racks for thread and patterns. The machine on a rolling table, along with a chair, fits neatly in a niche beneath shelves.

Hobby nook, *opposite,* was built at the end of a wide hallway where shelves extend from floor to ceiling, enclosed by double-hinged doors. Here, supplies for gift-wrapping and Christmas bauble-making are stored; the same scheme might serve a craftsman of another sort.

MARIS

MARIS

Film show gear, *above,* is concealed in the home of two amateur photographers except when in use. Screen is recessed in living room ceiling; slides and film hide in closet.

GUERRERO

Cleaning closet, *above,* holds every kind of help the tidiest housewife could want: a shelf, hooks, a revolving stand, plastic door-hung bins.

Outdoor clothes, *below,* find a spot next to the back door (and by the milk delivery slot). Metal trough holds boots; slats help to air wet coats.

STOLLER

ECKERT

277

2   MAYA

1   GRIGSBY

3   GRIGSBY

4   GRIGSBY

1 A woman's lingerie closet consists of two ranks of drawers lacquered in fresh, cool colors; up top, a compartment for extra pillows and a night coverlet.
To hide all: pair of double-hinged doors.

2 The work closet of an industrial designer is a beautiful design itself, with supplies carefully filed and color coded.

3 Beauty equipment fills an under-counter cabinet in a woman's dressing room that holds devices for skin, hair and hand care.

4 Sheets and towels in many patterns are stored in a linen closet lined in white vinyl and embroidered with butterflies.

5 Keys hang behind a little door, clearly labeled, making frantic searches for ways into storerooms and suitcases obsolete.

6 Household tools are often required in daily living. But a trip to the family workshop can be a chore, so an extra set hangs back of a kitchen door in easy reach.

7 Shallow shelves are made to do the work of storing pillows by attaching leather belt straps to the shelf edges.

8 A household file center occupies a whole closet, with colored cardboard stacking files, a pull-out Parsons table below, a chest and small drawers under the table.

9 A shallow five-shelf medicine chest has no wasted space. This one, recessed in a wood-paneled wall, has a louvered door.

10 A linen closet's folding and sorting shelf is made of two panels joined with a piano hinge. Outer panel folds up.

11 A multi-faceted collection of art, antique artifacts and curiosa, displayed on a rotating basis, spends its resting time in bins and portfolios of a special closet.

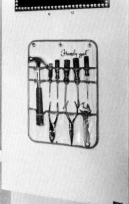

5

STOLLER STOLLER

6

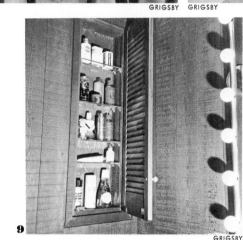

7

GRIGSBY GRIGSBY

8

9

GRIGSBY GRIGSBY

10

11

MASSEY

Chapter 10

PERSONAL TREASURES

LIVING WITH THE THINGS YOU LOVE

Because "the world is so full of a number of things," we begin choosing and bringing some of them home when we are tiny children. It may be a fistful of wilted dandelions, a few shells or shining pebbles, a bit of pale blue eggshell found under an apple tree. Thus early do we express our deep-rooted instinct to surround ourselves with things we love. As we grow older and more selective, we raise our sights from a striped pebble to a malachite box, from a tattered copy of *Peter Rabbit* to a first edition of *Pickwick Papers*. But the basic hunger to acquire and live with special possessions that appeal to us does not change.

What people collect and what they cherish vary as widely as individual tastes and temperaments. The most be-

loved objects in a house may have absolutely no appeal or value for anyone but the owners, or may be intrinsically rare and beautiful. The significance of personal treasures can be rooted in sentiment, aesthetics, recalled experience, whatever. But when people gather the things they love most around them, their houses become a true extension of themselves and as individual as their signatures.

Some of us are attracted to unrelated objects whose common denominator is decorative appeal. Others develop specific interests, become knowledgeable about them and gradually assemble one or more collections of paintings, sculpture, books, music. But all wise seekers and finders have one thing in common: they enjoy

living with their treasures on an intimate, everyday basis. They want to read their books, look often at their pictures or ornaments, fill their rooms with music, pick and arrange the flowers from their garden. All of which requires a great deal more planning than merely making space for things. It means giving them a setting where they not only look at home and at ease but can also be truly enjoyed for what they are. For example, books should be placed with regard for the room as an entity, but also be readily accessible. Again, a grouping of intriguing items should enhance its surroundings and be easy to examine, too. The secret is to use the things you love to give your house new and provocative dimensions as well as very private delight.

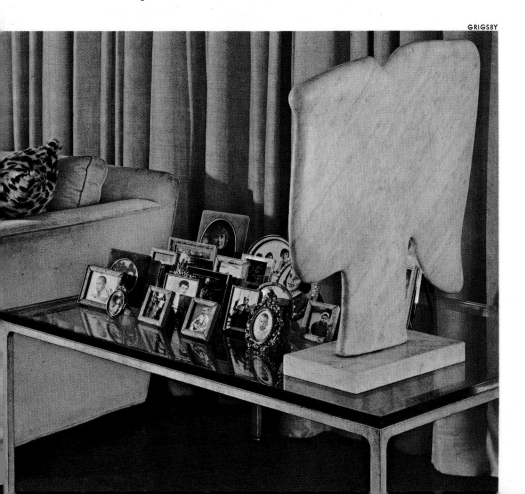

GRIGSBY

Family photographs, *left,* are grouped together on a low table in a master bedroom. A personal gallery in miniature, it offers no apology for its sentimental appeal. Exciting contrast: an avant-garde marble sculpture.

A congenial company, *right,* of loved objects and plants, surrounds a table tucked into the corner of a glassed-in porch. Brick walls set off colorful serving pieces, a gilded cherub, an old-time chest, a painting. Above eye level: treasured panels of stained glass. At dusk, soft light filtering through the leaves sets everything swimming in an opalescent radiance which the collectors also cherish.

GRIGSBY

PAINTINGS AND SCULPTURE

TO SURROUND YOU WITH BEAUTY

Great art speaks for itself. It establishes and maintains its own stature independently of environment. But most of us cannot collect masterpieces. We acquire pictures and sculpture that we love, want to live with and look at every day. How we display them is a creative act that calls for a sympathetic imagination and a sensitive eye. Scale is important. A small print is cast adrift on a large expanse of wall and a little figure gets lost in a maze of unrelated objects. Well-planned groupings make their point collectively, yet each item keeps its individuality. Large pictures should have space around them and usually look best with a base, such as a mantel, dado or low chest under them. Dominant sculpture should be placed where it can be seen freely from all sides. Concern yourself primarily with the positioning of your pictures and sculpture rather than with their suitability to a particular color scheme or furniture arrangement. Everyone who has ever moved knows that his artistic treasures have a way of triumphing in any setting if they are properly placed.

A glorious collection, *left,* receives the focus it deserves when every treasure is proudly displayed in distinctive—but low-keyed—surroundings. Plain white walls and a soft-spoken Persian silk rug from the 19th century are counterpoints for masterly 20th-century paintings and ancient finds. A bronze sculpture, dramatized by elevation on a handsome pedestal, is prelude to a procession that begins on the low marble bench with a Japanese figure and ends—some thousand years later—with a collage in a shadow box. Interior design: Armand Bartos.

LEONARD

PRIMOIS/PINTO

Bracketed grouping, *above,* of early Chinese sculpture and porcelains on a cinder block wall in a garden room, is carefully spaced but looks unselfconscious and delightful. Chunky wood brackets of various shapes and sizes set off the individual pieces. Philodendrons climb up the wall and across the raftered ceiling to frame this unusual, fine collection in graceful greenery.

Plotted arrangement, *left,* of pictures hung above a dado, patterns the high walls of an otherwise patternless living room. The asymmetrical composition cleverly includes a doorway that frames more of the collection in the room beyond. Plain curtains, low furniture and bare floor combine to focus full attention on the many works of art. Interior design: George Huet.

Inspired mélange, *right,* of the old and the new, gives a very efficient kitchen the romantic aura of an old Dutch interior. The doorway was fashioned from an 18th-century Bavarian cupboard. Around it and artfully hung to include it is a collection of old oils, and three mirror pictures (in a vertical group). All were brought together by a collector who believes in living easily with his superb treasures. The magnificent portrait is as much at home with old folk pottery and a tiled dado as with the very modern island work center that harbors a stainless steel sink.

BOUCHER

PERSONAL TREASURES
PAINTINGS
AND SCULPTURE

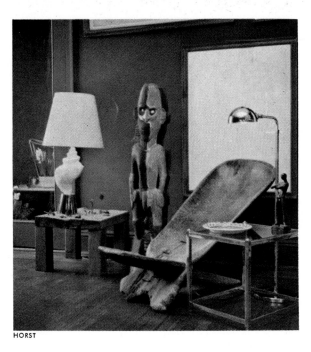

HORST

Paintings of heroic scale, *right,* demand giant backdrops and, almost always, solid backgrounds to set them off. For one powerful canvas that can be enjoyed from any angle, a bedroom ceiling proves a marvelous foil. For other compelling paintings: the serenity of glossy brown walls, neat window panels and one brown-patterned fabric.

Treasures that span ages, *left,* are imaginatively grouped in front of an intense blue wall which plays up the sharply contrasting silhouettes. In subtle balance: a contemporary drawing and lamps, a New Guinea carving, an African chieftain's chair—archaic, still regal.

Tremendous aesthetic variety, *below,* calls for precise placement to give each painting, drawing and sculpture its due. In a living room where works of art surround you, unity is achieved in several ways: frames are simple; pictures form a clean line below the ceiling and on the sides, making the wall itself a huge mat for all; one large sculpture dominates the space around it, including the boldly checked floor.

FAVORITE BOOKS

**TO COMPANION YOU
WHENEVER
YOU NEED THEM**

SHULMAN

Everyone collects books of one kind or another. The point is how to live with them most companionably and harmoniously. Luckily, filled bookshelves create a random pattern that is decorative, warm and suited to almost any room. Ideally, bookshelves should be located where you can read in comfort—in a living room, a study or a bedroom. If space is a problem, put the books you want to use often in the most convenient place and install shelves elsewhere, possibly in several spots, for the overflow. Books can look at home in a dining room, a hall, an unused cranny under the stairs or in some other area. Always make sure, however, that you have a good light near them for reading titles. Books of average size require shelves only about 8 inches deep; you will need deeper ones, of course, for outsized volumes. Since height varies so much, adjustable shelves are a sensible investment. Built-in shelves look best if they fill a clearly defined area, between corners and windows, for example. Open-ended shelves can vary in length and are more flexible if you wish to create a composition with them. It is always wise to build more shelves than you need so that, as books accumulate, you will have room for them. In the meantime, any open spaces can be used to display decorative objects, and the wall behind built-in shelves can be greatly enhanced by covering it with pattern or color.

Wall-to-wall bookshelves, *left,* transform a balcony into an intimate library overhanging a lofty living room. The comfortable browsing spot includes a desk, easy chairs. Dark wood shelves complement the ceiling drama. Architect: O'Neil Ford. Interior design: Weldon Sheffield.

A sizable wedge of space, *above,* under open stairs, is used for open-end bookshelves that conform to the irregular shape of the wall: the bottom shelves are the longest. Interior design: J. R. Davison.

End wall in an upstairs hall, *bottom, left,* becomes useful and decorative when fitted with shelves that harbor books-to-take-to-bed.

Ceiling reach of bookcases, *below,* above enclosed cupboards, gives dramatic unity to the study end of a multipurpose room. A built-in desk within fingertip reach of wanted volumes is superbly lit by a glass wall. Architect: Joseph Esherick. Interior design: Andrew Delfino.

BEADLE

STOLLER

LYON

GRIGSBY

Diminutive library, *left,* with nothing too weighty in its makeup, fits into a flower-lined dining room. To make the look light and bright, shelves are painted white like the woodwork, and divided here and there by uprights that keep books in small groups. Many of the volumes are given protective jackets in striped paper or a documentary print. Interior design: Eleanor Ford.

Backless trio, *below, left,* of high bookcases, lets a guest room's pretty wallpaper show through. A pleasant choice of books is combined with flowers, bibelots and a bit of desk space. For reading pleasure: an easy chair with a lamp on one side and a patio on the other.

Shelves to the rafters, *right,* frame tall glass doors to the terrace of a weekend house. Located where the action is, the wall-climbing library encourages browsing. A necessity here: the tall ladder.

Inviting corner, *below, right,* in which to curl up with a good book, is built midway along the wall of a vast living room. Angled into the room, one of the two ceiling-high stacks serves as a space divider designed to create a sense of coziness. The well-stocked shelves are in warm contrast to surrounding white, beige and wood tones. For the reader, the luxury of a chaise—this one an antique turned so its gracefully curved frame can be seen from all sides. Interior design: Michael Taylor.

End-to-end array, *far right,* of books, fills almost an entire wall opposite the fireplace in a collector's living room. Interrupting the abundance of shelves: a flush, vertical panel of mirror reflects part of the room as well as a handsome porcelain urn; a niche above the double doors holds a superb jar.

LYON

STOLLER

LEONARD

CHERISHED COLLECTIONS

TO SAVOR ON MANY LEVELS

Almost everybody collects something—because it is a natural human instinct and a lot of fun. Whether you are serious or lighthearted about it, you will not be happy to hide your treasures once you get them home. Your prides and joys may be prints or pebbles, old glass or old keys, Lowestoft or ladles. Whatever they are, display them unabashedly where they can be seen, enjoyed and admired. If they are a pleasure to handle and not too fragile, place them where your guests can enjoy their tactile as well as their visual values. Any collection of medium-sized or small objects takes on importance when it is arranged in an attractive group rather than scattered piece by piece about the house. Often, very diverse things make a harmonious whole; those of one kind invariably enhance each other. A wall, a cabinet, open shelves, a wide windowsill, a tabletop—can become the setting for a collection. To create a pleasing composition, experiment until your eye tells you that you have achieved it.

Meticulous grouping, *right*, of bold paintings, Portuguese apothecary jars, green opaline boxes and small Indian bronzes, compose one marvelous assemblage in an entrance hall. Even the lamp is carefully positioned. Tiny engravings and little clocks persuade one to take note of every detail. Interior design: Evelyn Jablow.

A heady array, *below*, of American Indian pottery stands out amid the treasures of collectors who adore variety. But they blend order with impact by keeping similar things together—pictures, books, pottery—yet combining all together in one display.

ECKERT

MAYA

MASSEY

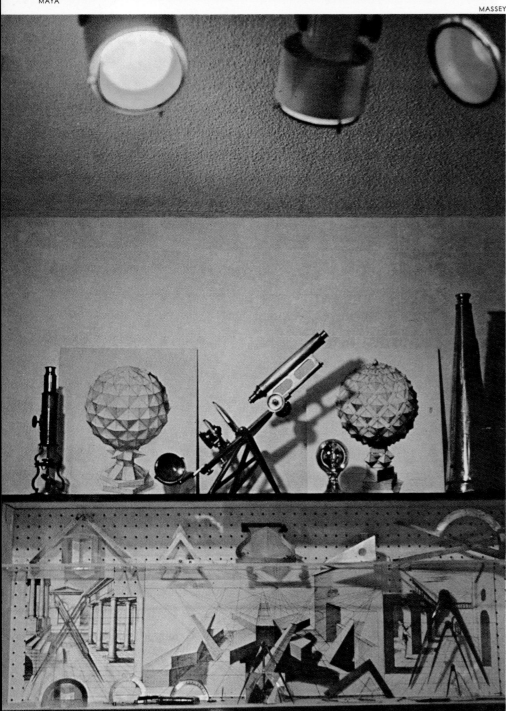

Niches for miscellany, *above,* make a satisfying
arrangement of diverse objects collected by a
teen-age boy. Mondrian-like divisions with
yellow edging bring unity. Interior design: Bill Lanyon.

Window's natural light, *left, top,* and a radiator
cover's length enhance a pretty spread of opaline.
The blue glow, concentrated in one area,
adds a sharp accent to the surrounding yellows
and greens. Interior design: Howard Perry Rothberg.

Clear-view case, *left, bottom,* with a glass front and
unobtrusive inside shelf, beautifully houses antique
instruments, from calipers to telescopes.
Fixed to a perforated board back—
and adding greatly to the overall design impact
—are many small Photostats of perspective drawings.

Playful mural, *below,* in a kitchen, brings a needed
telephone, clock and electric light switch plate
into the act, along with a giant needlework
daisy, ancient keys, an old fish scale, a cigarette roller.

YEE

YEE

MAYA

Two-surface arrangements, *above,* artfully combine porcelain treasures with little, unrelated objects. To link the table array to the collection on the wall shelves, the tabletop was stenciled in a Delft tile pattern. Interior design: Doris Dessauer.

The whitest of planking, *left, top,* brings out the nuances of old ironstone platters, each subtly different in its whiteness. No vibrant color distracts from the collection; the room gains warmth solely from wood tones. Interior design: John Dickinson.

An expansive wall, *left, bottom,* is patterned in high relief with a vast collection of keys. To space them evenly, the larger keys were placed first, and then the smaller ones were arranged around them. Interior design: Richard McKay of Jessup, Inc.

Writing table, *below,* affords a keen collector of sparkling paperweights frequent opportunities to enjoy them at close range. Light from a nearby window turns the myriad colors into unending rainbows.

GRIGSBY

KERTESZ

A TREASURY OF FLOWERS

TO GLADDEN YOU AND YOUR HOUSE THE YEAR 'ROUND

Old tea caddy brims with a short-stemmed nosegay that has a casual, just-gathered look.

Flowers can add lilt and loveliness to a room or they can be merely another accessory. The difference lies in how you use them. Studied arrangements are static; they lack the garden-and-field naturalness of uncontrived bouquets. Which does not mean that a spontaneous look is easy to achieve; it requires practice and imagination. But once mastered, the art of fixing flowers with simple grace will give you endless pleasure. Experiment in various ways. For example, put an armful of lilacs in a silver wine cooler for a lavish look, or one lavender tassel in a tiny bottle for minute perfection. Mix bold and delicate blossoms; add sprigs of mint for another aroma. Be inventive about containers. All kinds of glasses work beautifully. So do pitchers, baskets or boxes with liners, bottles and crocks, given the right blooms and the right setting. Copper, brass, and tin can be as flattering to flowers as silver ever was. On these pages, garden flowers take their transient magic to every part of the house. On the next pages: wild flowers, berries, grasses—put together in fresh, unstudied ways.

Massed roses, from buds to overblown, smile from a tin-lined basket on a coffee table.

A few pale flowers enhance a little grouping of vivid blue glass.

Green medicine bottle on a low table sets off the beauty of two perfect blooms.

Three tiny delights are placed with artful care to create one enchanting arrangement.

An overflowing basket, looking as if it had just been carried in from the garden and set down on a small table, holds an exuberant, summer-scented bouquet.

Cheerful splash of tulips and candytuft in clear crystal greets visitors in a front hall.

Big vase on the floor holds an explosive spread of color in front of a long window.

Airy, colorful mix of simple and elegant blooms spreads wide at the top.

Pyramided tiers of nasturtiums, daffodils and sweet peas are surrounded by pieces of glazed earthenware.

Glass tumbler makes much of pansies' pretty faces and their stems.

Solid cluster of many different short-stemmed blossoms and trailing ivy conceals the vase.

Heady hyacinths nested in a cabbage tureen are a perfumed pleasure on the coffee table in a living room.

Sweet surprise on a bathroom soap dish: a tiny jar of daffodils and one peach-toned tulip.

Wide milk crock is crammed with vibrant hues set off by its heavy simplicity.

WILD FLOWER ARTLESSNESS

Wild flowers are waiting to be found, picked and fixed in casual, airy bouquets. On your rambles, carry a light container of water to keep your blooms fresh until you get them home. Some will droop and not recuperate; some will last only a day. But many have staying power plus a gay and guileless charm.

Elfish snuffbox of onyx on a gleaming table bursts with the joy of wild asters, tiny but varied.

Breezy urnful of goldenrod, wild asters, ferns, a gathering of leaves, fans out on a patio floor.

Garden basket carries mountain laurel from a personal bit of woodland to a terrace table.

Antique silver bowl enthrones cardinal flowers and maidenhair ferns found on a mossy bank.

Spikes of bright berries, including orangey viburnums, pack mirth in a willow basket.

Innocent handful of Canada thistle and curving millet grass graces a butterfly-patterned bowl.

SUN-BLEACHED TAWNINESS

Feathery plumes and beach grass, moonpennies, dried flowers, seed pods clinging to their stems—all can be combined many ways for a staccato or soft effect. The subtle, neutral coloring has an understated distinction that delights the eye for weeks. Change is also pleasing, so make new bouquets regularly.

Crowning glory atop a pedestal combines wild sprays with more civilized baby's breath (which dries like a dream).

Beach grasses and golden seed heads of dried dock spark a white wall.

Silvery cooler sets off meadow finds plus non-grass "beads" from the florist's.

Feathery plumes of pennisetum and horsetails are flamboyant in a tin washtub.

Two vases, one almost a small echo, hold whiskery bursts of dry dune grass and wheat.

Flare-up of grasses and rushes, five feet tall, fills a high window with arrow-sharp accents. 299

MUSIC AT YOUR FINGERTIPS

TO PUT HOME IN TUNE WITH YOUR MOOD

Music at home has become such an important part of 20th-century life that in many families a musical instrument or a collection of records actually tops the list of things people love to live with. But since music is an auditory pleasure, making room for it tends to be somewhat more complicated than finding places for paintings, books and collections of objects whose appeal is primarily visual. The joy of playing is inevitably influenced by mundane considerations such as convenience, comfort, good light. The joy of listening can be enhanced or marred by the physical state of the instruments and the arrangement of the furniture. The equipment that produces the best sound is not always the most beautiful to look at—it begs to be minimized visually or actually concealed. And recorded music—tapes as well as disks—calls for adequate storage where it can be well preserved and well organized within easy reach.

Placing Pianos and Organs

Where to put the piano is a point that can set off a flurry of claims and counterclaims in any family. If the only consideration is the well-being of the piano, the answer is simple: put it anyplace in the house where it can stand against an inside wall, well away from windows, radiators, fireplaces or other sources of fluctuating temperature and humidity. But that, of course, ignores the well-being of the pianist, as well as the looks of the room and any other purpose for which it might be used. When you juggle all the pertinent factors, one or two will almost certainly have to give. Just where you can afford to compromise depends on two sets of variables which you should consider.

The first concern is who will play the piano and why. If it happens to be a young student, then his comfort—both physical and psychological—is crucial. A child is apt to practice much more willingly in a lighthearted informal room with lots of daylight. An adult who plays primarily for his own amusement will also play more often

(Continued on page 302)

YEE

A made-to-order spot for a home organ is a niche created by built-in bookcase cabinets that minimize the instrument's back-to-front dimensions. The painting hung on panel above niche draws the eye upward and keeps the not-very-tall organ from looking squatty.

An ideal spot for a grand piano to be played by an adult is the inside corner of a room, away from windows and radiators. When playing for his own enjoyment, the pianist has a pleasant view, yet he need not turn his back on guests. Interior design: Melanie Kahane.

GRIGSBY

LEONARD

Two connecting rooms, *above*—or one large L-shaped space—offer an
excellent place for a grand piano where the rooms merge. Here a
sheer curtain makes a visual backdrop for the piano
without actually blocking the sound. Interior design: Virginia Whitmore Kelly.

Two grand pianos, *top, above,* take up less room than you might imagine
when they are the same size and placed curve-to-curve.
(Children take much more interest in the piano
when they can play with a parent or friend.) Interior design: James Amster.

where he feels at ease, but for him night
lighting may be more important. If someone
in the family frequently performs for guests,
the position of the piano in relation to comfortable chairs and sofas has to be considered. And if he is sometimes joined by
string players, there must be room enough
near the piano for *their* chairs and music
stands—and good light for everybody. A
piano used mainly for parties, however, may
be tucked into any out-of-the-way corner,
since it is to be heard rather than listened
to—and not necessarily watched.

The second set of variables concerns the
type of piano and the size and shape of the
room. Obviously, a grand consumes the
most floor space, but it does not have to
be placed against a wall. In fact, if the room
is large enough, the best location on all
counts might be dead center, or even the
open space where two connecting rooms
merge, provided traffic is not blocked.

Placing Uprights

Vertical pianos take up less floor space
but, except for those of special design, always require wall space. A full-sized upright
—the 48-inch studio piano that many musi-
cians feel is second in tone only to a grand—
may also seem large in scale compared to the
room's other furnishings.

An organ, too, must be placed against a
wall. Although not as tall as a studio upright, it is considerably deeper and looks
best in a niche—real or created by furniture
—that will minimize its depth. Leave a small
space between the back of an upright piano
and the wall so the wall can act as an additional sound reflector. As a rule, it is a good
idea not to stand a home organ on bare
floor, since it will tend to bounce back the
sound and set up unpleasant reverberations.
In most cases, a piano is all right on bare
floor—as it is on the concert hall stage—but
in a room with very hard surfaces, you may
find you need to stand the piano on a rug.

How to House Stereo

Development of the transistor has led to
so much "miniaturization," that there is no
(Continued on page 304)

MARIS

GRIGSBY

GRIGSBY

HORST

Panels of caning, *above,* across the back of this rosewood and steel upright, make it possible to use the piano as a room divider, a particularly welcome arrangement in a large room with big windows and little wall space.

Flower patterns, *top, left,* gaily painted on a white lacquered piano, blend in with the flowered fabric that covers most of the furniture. Mirror behind the piano seems to open up the wall. Its smooth, hard, sound-reflecting surface is compensated for by wall-to-wall carpet, lots of upholstered chairs.

A wall of books, *top, right,* makes an excellent frame for an upright and seems to reduce its size. The simple ruse of leaving a gap in the three lower shelves created a shallow niche that gives the piano an integrated look.

A child's own room, *left,* is great for a practice piano. To diminish the scale of this studio upright, it was painted white like the wall, then broken up by panels of color. Interior design: Virginia Whitmore Kelly.

such thing today as a room too small for stereo. True, avid music buffs still prefer (and probably always will) to buy every single component, small or large, individually. But however glorious their sound, such assemblages tend to sprawl over considerable space and are not very pretty to look at. They are best tucked away in a closet or cabinet, to be heard but not seen.

You can get excellent sound today, however, from a four-piece modular or "packaged" lineup consisting of tuner-amplifier, a record player and two speaker systems. Since each of these units is neatly encased and connected to its partners with a minimum of wiring, many people are happy to keep them in full view on open bookshelves. Even more condensed is the three-piece "compact," consisting of tuner, amplifier, record player and sometimes a cassette player—all in one box—plus two speaker systems. These, too, may be left in full view, although some people would rather conceal their music equipment no matter how neatly it is encased.

Choosing Cabinets

When you go shopping for a cabinet to house a music system, there are a few points to look out for. One is the depth. A shelf 15-inches deep is needed for modular components and is adequate for compacts that have the controls at the side (those with controls at the front are deeper). Antique armoires make beautiful cabinets for music systems, having the advantage that you can place the record player on a conveniently waist-high shelf; the disadvantage is they are too narrow to house more than one speaker —the other must be placed elsewhere.

If a long low cabinet would fit your room better, you must decide whether you prefer the type that opens at the top (as some especially designed for music do) or at the front only (which means you will have to

(Continued on page 306)

GRIGSBY

GRIGSBY

GRIGSBY

Wall-to-wall music center, *above,* leaves no trace of its existence when all the walnut doors and drawers are closed, *left.* Among the built-in cabinets and drawers are deep files for music scores, shelves for reference books, compartments for records and tapes, cubicles for stereo components. At end near piano, tape recorder was built into compartment with drop-down shelf that serves as a handy work surface. Interior design: Henry Robert Kann.

Working music room, *right,* is furnished with all the equipment a composer needs for his creative hours, yet remains a pleasant place for playing and listening. A display of framed prints and manuscripts raises the visual stature of the small upright piano to that of the book and record wall where 10,000 records are stored. To make the most of his space, the musician bought cartons of empty six-sleeve albums, then added two more sleeves to each.

MILLER

YEE

YEE

stoop to put on records). If you plan to have the cabinet house the speakers as well as the player and amplifier, you would do well to pick one with sliding doors that can be left open without getting in the way.

Placing Speakers

Stereo speakers should be 6 to 10 feet apart, depending on the size of the room. Be careful not to separate them too much or you will get a hole in the middle that will result in choppy, disconnected sound. If the speakers are too close, however, you will not get the sense of space and depth that is the object of good stereo. Keep them at seated eye-and-ear level if possible—at least 3 or 4 feet off the floor. In a concert hall, if you can see the performers well, you can usually hear well, and this holds true for music speakers at home. If they are too near the floor, chairs and tables in the path of the sound will obstruct the high tones and the sound will tend to boom and become unnatural.

Placing the speakers in the corners of a room often produces excellent results. Bass notes radiate from a speaker in all directions, so by placing the speaker in a corner, you channel them into a more limited area and emphasize the deep, throbbing tone that gives the music its richness.

In a long narrow room, mounting the speakers on one of the short end walls tends to emphasize the resonances of the room, while mounting them on a long wall may diminish the bass. The best plan is to try both and judge which sounds most natural to your ears, which is, after all, the best criterion for musical sound. Settle on what pleases you most, for individuals' ears react to music with astonishing variations of acuteness, and the sound in your living room should be among your greatest personal joys.

Cabinets flanking a fireplace, *above,* house a complete music system, including a pair of speaker systems.
On the left side, directly under books, are pigeonholes for tapes which can be hidden by tambour doors, and below them, one speaker system with fold-back doors. Long shelf (also with tambour doors) under books at right holds tuner, amplifier, preamplifier. In lower cabinets are tape recorder and pull-out record player, *left,* and the second speaker system.

Four-part music wall, *above, top,* is partly closed, partly open. Doors can conceal two speaker systems (far left and far right), all other components and record storage.

A complete music center, *above,* contains everything a concert cellist needs for his profession, including storage for his instruments. TV mounted on swivel base can be hidden by hinged doors. All else—tape and record players and an entire music library—disappears behind sliding doors. Panels of upper doors are covered with linen.

Built-in speakers, *far left,* above TV-music center and bar, are concealed by wooden grille doors. When closed, wall is a smooth sweep of hemlock. Architect: Joseph Esherick.

Revolving cabinet, *left,* houses speakers behind a stretch of orange fabric. When reversed, music components disappear, and back of cabinet covered with the same fabric becomes a flush panel in wall. Interior design: Marvin C. Sharpe.

307

Chapter 11

PERSONAL EXPERTISE
The sure knowledge
that
you can enhance
each room
in the right way

HOW TO ASSESS ANTIQUES

BEADLE

Like any safari, antique hunting calls for certain preparations: assembling the right equipment; training in awareness; learning how the quarry may be hidden or disguised by possessive and often eccentric keepers. You could easily spend years at this, but for amateur collectors here is a short course in the art of finding and buying antiques that are worth their price.

Obviously, the easiest, least expensive way to acquire antiques is to inherit them. But to a born collector, this is no fun at all. It eliminates the joy of a bargain.

Begin by boning up on the primary laws of antique hunting. *Comfort:* Wear clothes and shoes that will allow you to bend, reach and grab with ease. If you need glasses for reading, wear them for antiquing. This is one sport in which vanity will get you nowhere. *Curiosity:* Always look up and down. Top shelves and floors may be crammed with delights you will miss at eye level. *Research:* Once you fall under the spell of a particular type of antique, read some books on the subject. The more you learn, the more fascinating the quest becomes. *Big dealer versus small dealer:* The bigger dealer is often cheaper in the long run. He carries a large stock and can afford to spread his profits, whereas a small dealer may try to make his whole day's profit from you. *Cleanliness versus messiness:* In the same vein, don't pay for housekeeping. You will do better in a disordered shop than in one where everything is spit-and-polished. Use your imagination. Think what a little wax polish will do. Be like a dealer: buy antiques rough; do some research and restore their splendor yourself. *Bravery:* Always ask the dealer to point out any damage. Most dealers are honest, but they are not fools. If you don't ask, they will not volunteer the information. Since many shops have poor light for either aesthetic or practical reasons, insist on inspecting things in strong daylight or carry a pocket flashlight for a close, careful look. *Sincerity:* If mere profit were the dealer's sole ambition, he would be in another business. Most dealers love antiques with a passion and would rather sell sympathetically to buyers who are sincere, giving them a good price, than earn a bit more in cut-and-dried transactions. Dealers have been known to refuse to sell an item to a customer who failed to display proper appreciation. Even when haggling, do so with (Continued on page 310)

HOW TO GO TO AN AUCTION

Veteran auctioneers, like croupiers and innkeepers, are apt to be astute students of life, grown wise in the practice of their trade. While they are content to see their older, more affluent customers bid up the price of a Tournai tapestry, they express a tender solicitude for the young, who must maneuver within the limits of a modest budget. Their advice to the married couple is simple and forthright: go to auctions together, examine the wares together and cast your bids together.

Throughout the year, auction galleries in the larger cities hold sales regularly, sometimes several times a week. These sales are announced in local newspapers. For the novice, just dropping in at a gallery and watching the progress of the bidding can be a pleasant pastime. At times, when important collections of antiques or works of art are sold, the sales are spectacular and exciting. More than one painting now in the National Gallery or the Metropolitan Museum of Art has at some time in the past come up for bidding at an auction house. And on rare occasions such outstanding works of decorative art as Paul Revere silver, Benjamin Randolph chairs and Imperial Chinese jades appear on the auction block. This is heady stuff, and prices can soar into the thousands. But at many an everyday sale, some amateur auction-goer has bought an object which, though not for the great collector or for the museum, lends distinction to his house.

Whether you go to the streamlined city gallery or to a country auction with camp chairs set up in the yard, by all means shed the attitude of the department-store shopper. Though you are buying through a retail outlet, the conditions of sale are unique. The auctioneer generally is not the owner of what he sells, but merely a broker who operates on a commission basis. All things are sold "as is," with "no exchanges, returns or refunds." Finally, all sales are strictly "cash and carry."

Before deciding to have a try at auctions, you should know what you are getting into. Pay visits to some of the better known galleries and scout around among smaller ones. Most good galleries will either make their advertisements fairly detailed or they will send announcements, on request, listing the general categories of things to be included in any one sale. Here is how one might read:

(Continued on page 311)

a subtlety that shows you "belong." *Precaution:* If your buy can break, take it with you or ask to have an outside firm pack and ship it. This is particularly important when traveling abroad since shipment home can be rough on delicate items, and most dealers, except for the very big ones, are not equipped to pack against breakage. Professional packing is well worth the small additional cost because insurance money can never compensate for shattered treasures.

Once out on the hunt,. your strategy should vary according to the kind of shop you are in. The junk shop, for instance, is the one place where it is wise to act ignorant —even more ignorant than you are. Since even with your limited knowledge you probably know more than the junk man does, do not show off by asking if this glaze is 18th century or that mirror is authentic Chippendale. He will not know, but your seemingly expert interest may boost the price. Do not go too far the other way, however. Calling something a dirty old broken-down chair will only arouse suspicion.

In the better establishments, the trick is to make the dealers think you know *more* than you do. Since they are apt to be rather knowledgeable themselves, your best strategy is reflective silence, broken only occasionally by a casual question or comment. If you make the right comments—even one or two—the dealer will assume there is more expertise behind your veil of reticence, and he may be more frank about the condition and worth of his wares. For example, when looking at a set of straight chairs, you might ask "No arms?" meaning, "There are no arm chairs to match?"

When Expertise Counts

Between Regency and early Victorian chairs, the chief design difference is the legs: saber-footed (splayed slightly) for the earlier period, rounded and turned for the later. If rounded, say, "It's a pity they're not saber-legged!" and the dealer will know you know they are not as good as they might be, and the price must drop accordingly.

Whatever the seeming condition of Sheffield or other plated silver, always ask, "Is it ragged?" Ragged means that a layer of modern silver plate has been applied quickly with a rag over the old silver where it has worn thin, possibly down to the base metal.

When you buy old Sheffield, don't be afraid to ask for a bill that clearly states the piece is in its original condition and has not been re-plated or ragged.

If you have found a lovely old urn that looks like antique Wedgwood, catch the dealer's eye and sigh, "Wouldn't you say this is an extremely good German reproduction?" Several German potters did copy Wedgwood designs, so if what you have found is authentic, the dealer will go to great lengths to prove it by showing you the markings that indicate authenticity.

It is naive to expect an old clock to work. In fact, you should be suspicious if it does, because that means you are paying for the cost of putting it in tick-tock condition rather than for its antique value. The big clocks are inscribed by the maker. If you must look at a clock for more than its beauty, have the innards fixed after you have bought it.

Do not expect old glass, including picture glass, to be regular or level. The lines and bubbles often found are called striations. Lament, "There doesn't seem to be any striation. Are you sure it's authentic?"

If you take antique hunting seriously, you must arm yourself with the right equipment. You need money, stamina, and three essential tools: a penknife; a pocket flashlight; a substantial straight pin, preferably a hat pin, lodged under your lapel or in the lining of your handbag.

Be an Expert

The penknife comes in handy when, from out of the jumble, you have fished a miracle in metal, plated with gold or silver. What you must find out is whether the plating is soft or hard metal—soft being worthless. Here is how you use your trusty blade: Stab the piece. If the knife goes easily into the brass, copper or lead-type foundation as if the plating were butter, let the piece pass. If you cringe at stabbing, simply flourish the knife while asking the dealer whether the plate is hard or soft.

In another shop, a fabulous old bowl comes to light, but you do not want to show your ignorance by asking the dealer whether it is pottery or china. If there is no strong light around, hold the bowl up and shine your flashlight behind it. The thickest china or porcelain will show a glimmer of light;

even the best earthenware is totally opaque.

While you may not care much whether an antique has been restored, you should pay less if it has. Your hat pin will not penetrate china but it will puncture plaster or glue repairs, however cleverly they have been made. On old carved frames, you can make a pin stand upright in the real wood but not in a part restored with plaster made to look like wood—no matter how hard you try. Should the dealer hover, ask right out if you may have a prod. If the frame is all wood, he will not mind. If it isn't, he will admit the restoration and charge less. For judging jade, the pin is indispensable. Real jade is harder than steel and cannot be scratched by a nail file, much less a pin.

Do not, however, let the fact that you can detect bits of restoration cloud your enjoyment of an antique. Most antiques—especially furniture—are restored to some extent. Perfect antiques are at a premium and extremely expensive. Therefore, some restoration should be accepted.

When negotiating the final price, it is ungallant to run down the condition or value of the item you are dickering for. Both you and the dealer lose face when you stoop to the level of character assassination. Simply be firm and poker-faced about the price you wish to pay, and don't deviate.

Price established, protect the value of your property by insisting that the bill of sale states categorically what the piece is, its actual age, the factory or place of origin and exact current condition. An accurate invoice is essential for tax purposes, for returning the item if for some reason you are displeased, for customs declaration if you have made your purchase abroad and for possible future resale.

If you are merely looking for the occasional modestly priced antique that is at once decorative and useful, small items in glass, china, pottery, pewter and wood are still plentiful. The revival of interest in Tiffany glass has boosted its market value tremendously, but 19th-century pressed glass and art glass are relatively inexpensive at the present time.

Finally, never buy anything simply because it is *old*. Age is not necessarily a synonym for beauty or even charm, and bad taste is by no means a recent development.

PERSONAL EXPERTISE

"American and European antique furniture from several estates; porcelains, glassware, clocks, mirrors, rugs and other furnishings."

If the listing sounds promising, be sure and note not only the date of sale but especially the dates of exhibition. The soundest advice for a would-be buyer is to examine the wares before they go on sale. By viewing them while they are on exhibit, you can take plenty of time to inspect and make up your mind. It can be disastrous to wait until an object is on the block, because the pressure of competitive bidding is likely to make a buyer reckless.

When you visit the auction rooms before the sale, arm yourself with a catalog, if there is one, and also with a notebook and pencil. The attendants will direct you to any listed object or lot you wish to see, and you will surely notice other things you had not thought of finding. Some galleries will oblige a prospective buyer by giving him an estimate of what a given object will bring, and if for any reason you are unable to attend the sale, they will place a bid for you. This procedure can be an intriguing gamble. If your proxy bid is exceeded, naturally you fall from the running. But if your bid not only tops the highest bid cast at the show but is actually well above it, most good galleries will award you the object at the first step-up above the final bid, thus enabling you to buy at a lower price than you were actually willing to pay.

Ordinarily, because you will prefer to attend the sale and bid in person, you should list in your notebook the lot numbers of objects upon which you have decided. If there are several lots which appeal to you, note possible alternates. Then, opposite each item, jot down the top offer you would bid for each lot. At this point, you should understand just how many items you are bidding for, because it is sometimes the custom of galleries to show only a sample of a great number of identical small objects. When, for instance, the entire contents of the old Ritz-Carlton Hotel were sold at auction, a New York newspaperman spied a couple of small smoking stands on the block. He bid for them—and won them. In settling up at the cashier's booth, he discovered to his dismay that he had actually bought over a hundred. Some lots consist of odd but related items.

At big city auctions, the buyer should expect to pay a fair price for an object for which there is competition. There is little real prospect of making a killing by discovering something that has escaped the expert amateurs or the shrewd dealers who make routine calls during the period of exhibition. The mere presence, however, of professional dealers should not dishearten the novice. On the contrary, because it is dealer practice to buy auction objects and then re-sell them at a profit in their own shops, they may point the way to an item worth fighting for.

Following the Bidding

Once you have sized up a collection and carefully noted the things that hold your interest, you are ready to face the auction itself. There is no hard-and-fast bidding pattern. Usually, the auctioneer himself will give the cue. Remember that he has the power to reject the first bid if he does not regard it as a worthy starting point. Yet, he is bound by law and custom to accept subsequent bids, providing they represent proper units of advance in price.

Where the value is substantial, bidding often goes along in the pattern of $10, $25 or $100 increments. But objects of lesser value may start at $2 or $5. A nod of the head or a wave of the hand is generally all that is needed to signify your willingness to advance the bid in the accepted unit.

You may cut your increase in half if you feel you are getting close to your operating limit. The auctioneer may just have said, "I have $90. Who'll say $100?" It is then quite acceptable to say $95, except that this acts as a flag to warn other bidders that you are backing off the scene, and that they may brazen you out.

Until you are fairly experienced, it is well to arrive early and sit away from the entrance, because the coming and going of others may either distract your attention at the wrong time or may prevent the auctioneer from seeing or hearing your signal. In the larger galleries, attendants accept and relay bids when necessary.

At times, the procedure at an auction seems almost automatic. Indeed, the majority of houses run sales at a fairly standard rate of sixty to seventy lots per hour. This actually serves to reassure the buyer, since in most well-managed sales every object or

group of objects is numbered, and these numbers are run off consecutively. It is therefore possible to know when a particular lot number will appear.

The bidding on individual lots, however, goes along very rapidly, and the novice is often shut out of the competition by the rocketing pace. You must be alert, with notebook in hand, so that you can jump into action when the right time comes.

After your moment of triumph, when you have placed a successful bid, the attendant will come up to you (unless you are known) and take your name and address and a cash consideration, usually 25 per cent of the purchase price, to seal the transaction. You should repeat to him the lot number, object and price, so that there can be no misunderstanding. In the rare instance where there has been some mistake, the auctioneer or his representative will put the object up again within a matter of minutes.

Getting your purchases home is your problem, not the gallery's. It is a great convenience to have a station wagon, although city taxicabs have had all sorts of improbable things hustled into them from auctions. For larger acquisitions, the auction house will recommend a dependable trucking firm.

Country sales, unlike city auctions, have a peculiarly unpredictable quality. They are usually conducted with no set pattern of bidding. If you can't wait, the auctioneer may put up your lot early.

Part of the fascination of auctions is to see collections endlessly formed and dispersed. You can, at any time, consign to the galleries for resale the treasures you have acquired. If you did not buy at a freakish price in the first place, your chances of getting a proportionate return on an auction purchase—even after paying the gallery's brokerage fee of 20 to 25 per cent—are decidedly favorable. It is possible, however, that the bidding will not reach a figure which you consider adequate. Should this happen, the only way you can regain your item is by bidding for it yourself, buying it back, and hoping for better luck at a subsequent sale. More often than not, however, you will keep and cherish your prizes. For in adding your own adventures to their history and particular appeal for you, they will become more personal and meaningful.

THE CARE AND SAFEKEEPING OF:

FURNITURE FINISHES

WICKER, RATTAN, BAMBOO, CANE AND RUSH

UPHOLSTERY

A beautiful mellow patina on fine furniture signifies years of rubbing, polishing and waxing. But the finishes on new furniture are remarkably durable. Regular dusting, an occasional washing and periodic polishing and waxing are all that is necessary to keep wood-tone furniture, old or new, in good shape. No one wax is good for all purposes, so read the label carefully to be sure you are using the proper type. To preserve sheen but avoid shine, use a cleaning polish with no silicone. Between waxings and polishings, any wood finish is improved by "massaging" (rubbing it with a soft, dry cloth), to remove smudges and help build up a patina.

Oil finishes take kindly to a periodic dry cleaning with mineral spirits before applying a new coat of warmed oil. Minor spots and rings may be erased by rubbing lightly with finest grade steel wool dipped in oil.

For the painted accent piece, the best care is the least: regular dusting with soft cheesecloth which is completely lintless and quite absorbent. Avoid the misguided use of polish, waxes or cleaners. If wax you must, do so not more than once or twice a year, using a thin coat of hard paste wax; dry thoroughly before buffing. Touch up minor spots and scratches on painted furniture with a very soft grease pencil or eyebrow pencil or hard paste shoe polish.

Lacquer finishes are not as sturdy as they look. Fingerprints and smudges show up easily, but a swish of a damp cloth followed by light buffing with a clean dry cloth will erase them.

When washing furniture, never overwet it, especially around the joints. Use warm water, a mild soap (with glycerin content) or mild detergent and a wrungout cloth or sponge.

True wicker is flexible, but it dries out unless it is "wet down" regularly. At least once a year, scrub it with a stiff brush, warm water and a mild soap, and set it out in the sun until it is bone dry. Then sand any roughness lightly with fine-grained sandpaper along the line of the wicker grain. Follow promptly with one or two coats of clear, thinned, white shellac. Wicker takes paint well; for best results and easy care, use a plastic-base paint.

Rattan is strong and flexible, but it survives best indoors or sheltered by a roof. If you subject rattan to outdoor exposure, frequent waxing (use a type with a natural wax base) and polishing are necessary to protect the finish and color from the elements.

Cane, the tough golden-tan bark of the rattan, is often used for chair seats. To tighten a cane seat that is beginning to sag, wash it with mild soap and water, rinse thoroughly and put it in the sun to dry. Be sure the seat is totally dry before you use it or it will soon sag again.

Rush, also used for chair seats, needs plenty of washing on a regular basis. Use a stiff brush, a mild soap, and water. Rinse well, and dry. A light coating of white shellac will protect the surface and anchor loose pieces. If a major break occurs, put the broken strand back in place and secure it with quick-drying plastic glue. When dry, shellac the entire seat.

Bamboo is a hollow tree growth, sturdy but not flexible. It requires nothing more than regular dusting, although wiping it off now and then with a damp sponge will freshen it, and an occasional light coat of wax that has a natural base will protect plain bamboo or the real tortoiseshell variety. But sponging and waxing may lift or dim a painted tortoise finish.

Any upholstered furniture will keep its looks longer if normal airborne dirt is not allowed to collect and linger on the surface of the fabric or become deeply embedded in the crevices. Regular cleaning with a whisk broom or vacuum-cleaner brush attachment gives far better results than infrequent intensive cleaning.

Keep a sharp eye out for sticky finger marks, oil stains, food spills. When the furniture is thoroughly dusted, treat the spots. Here are a few upholstery cleaning tips which are easy and safe for all fabrics: 1. Absorbent powders (cornstarch, fuller's earth, French chalk) remove fresh grease spots. Apply fairly thickly, leave on for several hours and then brush off. 2. Dry-cleaning fluids remove greasy soil. Always use in a well-ventilated room, and read directions on the label first. But never use a dry cleaner on furniture padded with foam rubber; it will soften and destroy the rubber. Use foamy or liquid upholstery cleaners instead; they do an excellent job. 3. Detergent-and-water solutions remove a great variety of food spills.

Before cleaning any upholstered piece, however, it is imperative to first test the fabric for colorfastness. Select an inconspicuous spot under the skirt or deep in a corner; try your cleaner to be sure it won't lift color off.

Immediate action is of course desirable on spots caused by foods or sticky fingers. These stains can often be removed with a solution of one part mild detergent (or commercial furniture shampoo) to four parts of warm water. Apply solution sparingly, using clean cloth and working from the outside of the stain toward the center. Rinse with a "dry-wet" clean cloth or sponge. Work quickly but gently; avoid too much rubbing and wetting.

MASONRY FLOORS

The perpetual joy of a masonry floor (including ceramic, mosaic or quarry tile, marble, terrazzo, slate, brick) is ease of maintenance. Clean water and a clean mop will do a splendid job. At most, you need nothing stronger than a mild detergent. Strong cleansers not only attack dirt but can also mar the surface of a floor, causing pits, scratches and abrasions.

A sealed surface will repel dirt, dust and moisture and resist acids, alkalies, oil, food, beverages, most inks, medications and puppy puddles. To properly preseal a new masonry floor, call in a trained person. Essential, however, to the care of even a sealed masonry floor is the prompt wiping up of spills before they become absorbed, and discolor or stain.

Generally speaking, waxing a masonry floor is superfluous. There is no point in waxing slate or unglazed mosaic tiles; it only masks their naturally beautiful matte texture. Nor does it make sense to wax glazed ceramic tile; it has its own permanent gloss. If you were to wax terrazzo, you would discover that the wax stays on top and "walks off" almost at once. Waxing does not enhance the already smooth surface of marble, and it turns white marble yellow. (To polish marble, call in an expert; the job requires patience, hard work and proper materials.) Some people wax quarry tile, building up a high gloss. But this obscures the soft, lustrous patina that is its most distinguishing feature.

If brick floors have a vapor barrier underneath, they may be safely sealed with varnish or shellac. If not, finish with a low-solid-contact wax or use nothing, and clean by sweeping. To remove grease spots from unsealed brick, scrub with a stiff brush and scouring powder or clean, wet sand.

RESILIENT FLOORS

Taking care of a resilient floor is fairly easy provided you know exactly what *kind* of floor you have. Periodic waxing, however, preserves the surface and emphasizes the luster of almost all resilient floors. For vinyl, vinyl-asbestos, vinyl-sealed cork, linoleum and natural cork, use a self-polishing wax or a solvent-base one that has to be buffed. A water-base wax should *never* go on natural cork. On asphalt or rubber tile, use *only* a water-base, self-polishing wax.

When a floor begins to look dull, it is time to wash it before you wax it again. For all floors except one of natural cork, use a mild detergent diluted with warm water as directed on the label. Apply the solution with a clean cloth, mop or polishing machine and scrub only where dirt has dug itself in. To remove stubborn spots, rub lightly with fine steel wool. Mop up the suds, rinse with clear, cool water, let the floor dry, and wax.

Instead of washing and waxing in separate steps, you can use a liquid cleaning wax, either the you-polish or self-polishing kind. Swab it onto the floor, leave there for a few minutes so the cleaning agent has a chance to dissolve the dirt, then wipe it up; a light residue of wax will dry shiny on the clean floor or have to be buffed, depending on the type you use.

All resilient floors (except perhaps natural cork) need to be stripped of wax on occasion. Twice a year should be often enough if you have been waxing in light coats. Use one of the specially made preparations for taking up old coats of wax. Proceed as described above for washing. Wax after the floor is totally dry.

Every day go over your floor with a broom, damp mop or vacuum cleaner, and wipe up any spills immediately.

WOOD FLOORS

If you inherit wood floors that have been well kept, try to find out *how* they were kept—and continue the routine unless it involves a water-base wax. This type must come up quickly or the floors will be ruined in time.

Floors that are in very bad shape should be smoothly sanded to the bone by a professional. Then at least two coats of penetrating sealer should be applied—transparent if the wood is handsome enough, otherwise stain-laden to alter or darken the color. Once sealed, a lightly trafficked floor may be waxed immediately. For heavier duty, it should be varnished, shellacked or lacquered first. A good varnish finish is tougher than shellac, more resistant to spilled water, less easily scratched. Lacquer dries very quickly and has a brilliant finish.

When the undercoating is thoroughly dry, it should be waxed. Paste wax applied with a floor polisher produces a lovely luster that, with occasional buffings, lasts for three months or longer. For a complete face-lifting, however, the old wax must be removed with turpentine or mineral spirits before applying a new coat.

Liquid waxes are easier to apply and, provided they do not have a water base, are good for floors and give a pleasant gleam. They clean as they go, removing the previous coat of wax, but must be used fairly frequently.

Once you have chosen a wax, stick with it. Remember: two thin coatings are far better than one thick coat.

For daily upkeep, use a dry mop or vacuum cleaner. Never use water on a wood floor unless essential, but if you must, work fast and get the floor dry quickly. Minor scratches and blemishes can usually be remedied with a brown crayon, a wax stick or brown shoe polish, then waxed to a shine.

PERSONAL EXPERTISE

THE CARE AND SAFEKEEPING OF:

RUGS AND CARPETS

REAL AND FAKE FUR RUGS

BOOKS

Although soil resistance and cleanability are engineered right into carpet fabrics today, cleaning on a regular schedule is essential to the good looks and longevity of rugs and carpets. The wear and tear of foot traffic is not half as hard on a rug's surface and construction as *dirt*.

"Loose" dirt, usually tracked in from outdoors, is bothersome but the least menacing. Given a chance, it will eventually dull rug colors and, because this type of soil is abrasive, it can wear down and cut the rug fibers. But it is easy to control; a quick, daily pickup with a vacuum cleaner or carpet sweeper plus thorough vacuuming twice a week will do the trick.

Hidden dirt is the deadliest kind. Adrift in the atmosphere, and oily, it is only visible when it settles on polished surfaces. When this airborne soil falls on fabrics and rugs, it is invisible, clings tenaciously, resists vacuuming and builds up to make rugs or carpets look dim and lifeless. Persistent home attention helps combat atmospheric dirt, which rarely penetrates more than one-third of the pile height. But before it goes that far, call in a professional cleaner.

The more rugs and carpets are vacuumed or swept (with a carpet sweeper, not a broom) the better they look. Vacuum and sweepers must be kept clean. Examine brushes regularly; they are usually removable for washing and taking off lint, threads, etc.

Most spots can be handled effectively with regular household agents or a spot and stain kit. Success comes with knowing what to do and doing it *promptly*. One word of caution: *never* use soap on a carpet or rug.

All soft floor coverings need periodic professional attention, at home or in a plant, by a reliable cleaner.

All furnishings that are made of fur need regular care at home plus periodic professional attention to restore their good looks and add to their longevity. Both short and medium-haired furs require approximately the same care—a periodic light vacuuming to remove surface oil, followed by brushing with a clean brush such as a standard scrub or a natural or nylon bristled dog-grooming brush. Never use metal on fur. Long-haired furs should not be brushed after vacuuming unless they have been treated first with a household cleaner that is recommended by fur experts for removing soil. If you have a back yard, an occasional airing is fine for fur. Otherwise, lift the corners of a fur rug, ripple the surface and let air circulate underneath. Shake a throw lightly as you would a fur coat.

After a year's use, a fur rug or throw should be cleaned professionally. Be sure the cleaner or furrier you pick is equipped to handle the work on his own premises, so that you will have recourse if the job is not satisfactory. Professional storage of furs is advisable in summer, with the possible exception of zebra.

Fake fur rugs and throws require little special care apart from a light shaking to remove loose dust and regular vacuuming to keep the pile fresh. When soiled, fake furs should be given a gentle washing in cold or lukewarm water with a mild detergent or soap, then dried out-of-doors away from direct sunlight. Do not dry-clean fake furs unless the maker recommends it. Wall-to-wall carpeting should be washed or cleaned commercially on the floor unless the label states otherwise. When buying fake furs, always be sure to get complete and accurate cleaning instructions.

Books respond best to regular care rather than to sporadic attention. Since the charm of open bookshelves cannot be denied, you must be prepared to pursue dust diligently. Using a soft, dry, clean cloth or soft brush, dust your books from back to front. Remove them as you do this, and wipe off the shelf, too, since any dust left there tends to work its way into binding and pages. Books may be vacuumed successfully, providing the brush attachment is properly handled, i.e., moved *lightly* across the top of the book. Never press down. Hardbound covers may be freshened up when dingy with art gum or a soap eraser.

The ideal temperature for the well-being of your books is 65 to 75 degrees with a relative humidity of 50 per cent. Direct sunlight or strong light of any kind is injurious to leather and cloth bindings alike—light dries out the former and fades both. Bookshelves should never be backed up to chimneys or placed over radiators—the book bindings will dry and warp in a very short time.

Never overcrowd your bookshelves; forcing books into place is fatal. They should stand loosely enough to be lifted out, not hooked off with one finger. Sturdy bookends, not books, are the only safe supports to hold up partially filled shelves.

Call in an exterminator if regular dusting reveals the presence of silverfish, moths or worms in any great number. Keep an eye out for mildew; if you find any, use one of the commercial products that absorbs moisture and hide it behind the books.

Steam heat is the arch enemy of fine leather bindings; they should be treated twice a year. "Lexol," a leather preservative, is endorsed by the British Museum and Brentano's bookstores.

COPPER, BRASS AND PEWTER

Basically, copper and brass are treated identically. The care of pewter is quite different. However, all metals have one point in common, i.e., they should be kept as dust-free as possible, because accumulated dust builds up into a greasy film which can be very hard to clean or polish off. Eventually, this layer of dirt will eat into the metal surface and cause permanent pitting.

Polishing solid metal cannot wear it out, but every time you polish plated copper or brass, you remove some coating. Look for a type of cleaner that is tarnish-resistant. Copper and brass cooking utensils cleaned with one of these products, then hung above a gas range, sometimes remain shiny for over two months with only soap-and-water washings after use. A time-saving trick for brass (not copper): Give it a weekly rubdown with a liquid ammonia cleaner poured on a piece of terry towel. Do not polish hardware; you may remove the finish.

Many copper and brass items are lacquered, which cuts down on polishing but prevents a patina from developing. Even lacquered pieces, however, should be dusted regularly. Note: Remove any lacquer from pots and pans before they are used the first time.

Today's pewter comes in a range of finishes from "antiqued" to a bright sheen. To keep it in perfect condition requires nothing more strenuous than dusting, plus an occasional washing to remove any slight darkening and fingerprints. Use a soft cloth with warm water and a mild soap or detergent; a soft bristle brush will reach crevices. Rinse, and dry at once to avoid watermarks. If new pewter tarnishes, it may need polishing with a good pewter or silver polish. Antique pewter, usually coated with dust, should be thoroughly washed to bring out its sheen.

STAINLESS STEEL, CHROMIUM AND ALUMINUM

Stainless steel is very easy to clean and keep clean. As it never tarnishes, it never needs polishing. It does not chip, break or dent, and is almost impervious to moisture, detergents and food acids. Flatware and hollow ware usually only require washing with a mild soap or detergent, and prompt drying to prevent the formation of water spots. Pots and pans may need pre-soaking to remove sticky foods; for stubborn cases, add baking soda to the soaking water. Never scrape stainless steel; it may damage the surface. When necessary, use steel wool or fiber pads or a mildly abrasive cleaner.

Chromium is a corrosion-resistant, non-tarnishing, hard, electroplated finish on alloy steel. Too-frequent cleaning and polishing with an abrasive will scratch chrome and may wear off a thin finish in a short time. A wiping with a slightly damp sponge is most effective and will not "lift" any of the plating. Periodic waxing of the chrome trim on your car or of chrome-plated outdoor furniture will protect the metal and retard deterioration.

Aluminum is a silvery, light, corrosion-resistant metal that is a favorite for pots and pans because it conducts heat quickly and evenly. Cast aluminum is usually of heavier gauge of thickness than sheet aluminum, but both are subject to stains that need prompt attention. To remove stains from a pan, fill it with enough hot water to cover them, and stir in two tablespoons of cream of tartar for every quart of water. Simmer for twenty minutes, let stand until cold, then scour with steel wool soap pads. More tips on aluminum care: Putting a very hot pan in cold water may warp it. Prolonged soaking in soapy water discolors a pan. Store pans uncovered; trapped moisture causes white spots.

SILVER

Silver can be easily scratched, but myriad tiny scratches give it a lovely patina. As patina only develops through use, and as daily washing and drying prevent tarnish from accumulating, use your silver every day. Treat it well; guard against careless loss of flatware and denting of hollow ware.

Certain foods tarnish or otherwise harm silver. Mustard, eggs and mayonnaise, for example, contain tarnishing sulfur. Salt has a corrosive action. So rinse all food particles off silver right after you use it. But never soak it; this dulls the finish and may loosen knife blades from handles.

If you wash silver by hand, do not wear rubber gloves; contact with rubber causes tarnish. Use a mild soap or a liquid detergent, then rinse. Dry each piece promptly and thoroughly, because even a trace of moisture picks up sulfur from the air. If you use a dishwasher, remove your silver as soon as the drying process has stopped. Never let it sit in a damp atmosphere.

Store silver when it is dry and cool in specially treated cloth bags or rolls, or in a lined drawer, chest or cabinet designed for the purpose. Most of these storage devices rely on cloth treated to prevent sulfur in the air from reaching and tarnishing silver.

How often your silver needs polishing depends on many factors. Do not immerse it in a chemical bath to remove tarnish quickly; you will dull the luster and bleach out desirable dark areas in designs. Use a traditional paste or liquid to clean and polish silver, or a tarnish-preventive type that leaves an invisible seal to ward off tarnish. A tarnish-preventive polish must be reapplied after several washings, and is more effective on pieces such as candlesticks that are dusted rather than those washed between polishings.

Note: *Since color and its use in decorating today are such important parts of this book, all references to color have been separately indexed. The general index covering all other topics in the book starts below, and the color index follows on page 320.*

COLOR INDEX